CHRIST IN HIS TIME AND OURS

Arthur A. Vogel

Sheed & Ward

Sheed & Ward™ is a service of National Catholic Reporter Publishing Company, Inc.

Library of Congress Cataloguing-in-Publication Data

Vogel, Arthur Anton.
    Christ in his time and ours / Arthur A. Vogel.
       p.   cm.
    ISBN 1-55612-555-0 (alk. paper)
    1. Jesus Christ—Person and offices. 2. Christian life—1960-
I. Title.
BT202.V59   1992   92-8034
232--dc20   CIP

Published by: Sheed & Ward
                    115 E. Armour Blvd. P.O. Box 419492
                    Kansas City, MO 64141-6492

To order, call: (800) 333-7373

Table of Contents

To
my family

The uncontrollable mystery on the bestial floor.

W.B. Yeats

1.

The Importance of Introductions

How we meet people is important. That is especially true of Jesus, for either his humanity or his divinity may be stressed in our introduction to him. There are reasons for emphasizing either, and each has been stressed from time to time through the centuries, but there are advantages to getting to know Jesus first in his humanity, as his disciples did. That is the best course to enable us to become his disciples today.

What greater influence is there in our lives than the people we have known? The personal influence of family members, friends, teachers, anyone we admire and want to be like, plays a singular role in the persons we become.

Events as well as people influence us, to be sure, but events in which we are involved—decisive events such as illness, injury, death, or accident—always involve the presence of other persons in some manner. If we are sick or injured, when we come to a new insight or achieve a goal, the influence and example of other people are always ingredients in the mix.

The influence of other people in our lives can be either positive or negative. Most infants are welcomed into the world in their families, but some are not. How we are received and treated by others in the first months of our lives gives us our first awareness of who we are and what we are worth. As we grow up, go to school, leave home, and become involved in the wider activities of the world, our friends and enemies, those who attract us and those from whom we flee, continue to influence us.

In addition to knowing people, how we get to know them, the manner in which we first meet them, is important. In some cases it is decisive: some introductions intrigue us; some put us off; still others may deceive us.

To be formally introduced to someone at a business meeting will do little to help us know that person for whom he or she really is. To have someone introduced by a formal title at a formal party tells us nothing at all about the person in his or her intimate, personal life.

Two young mothers, meeting each other while watching their children on the playground, will know more about each other after the first hours of a first meeting than diplomats know about each other at the end of a week's negotiations. It takes time to get to know someone as a person. We may first meet someone formally who later becomes a close friend, but the friendship will develop only as formal roles disappear and are replaced by spontaneous relations. What two people freely do in their spare time is more significant for their personal relationship than their formal titles.

Formal introductions, as we have indicated, are of little help in enabling us to know a person. Titles give no intimate information. People we know only by title, the president of a country, a governor, judge, professor, actor or actress, often surprise us when we meet them in person. They are not as different from us as the aura of their reputation leads us to believe. A big reputation, for example, leads people to expect a person very different from them to bear it. We are surprised at how short a famous person is; we anticipate looking up to him or her not just socially but physically.

It is unfortunate, but true, that the circumstances under which we first meet someone may actually keep us from meeting the person. We may be put off by appearances that are quite misleading, and what other people say about a person, even though it is offered with the best of intentions, may make the person seem unattractive. An introduction thus becomes a deterrent to our getting to know the true person to whom we are introduced. Two people may know the same person in very different ways.

As with other people, how we first meet Jesus has a lot to do with the Jesus we know—or do not know. It is important to meet the right Jesus, that is, the real Jesus, the right way. There are options. Jesus can be met in different ways. He can, for example, be met in what might be called, to continue the distinctions we have been using, a formal manner or an informal manner. We know about Jesus and have our first introductions to him only through those who claim to know him before us; that means our knowledge of Jesus has a dependence on the experience of others before we can have our own experience of him. How others choose to introduce him to us initially determines the only Jesus we can know.

We may have a formal or informal introduction to anyone, but with Jesus the distinction has a special significance. Christian faith professes Jesus to be truly God and truly human. Accordingly, when we are first introduced to him, the introduction may begin with either his divinity or his humanity. What is commonly known as high Christology begins with Jesus' divinity, and what is known as low Christology begins with his humanity. The presentation of Jesus in the Gospels of Matthew, Mark, and Luke begin with Jesus' humanity, although Mark proclaims Jesus to be the Son of God in his first sentence. John, on the other hand, begins his Gospel with the Word of God, the Word who is one with God and by whom everything which is made was made, and who was sent by the Father to become flesh and dwell among us in Jesus of Nazareth.

In the early church, so-called high Christology was especially associated with the theological thought of Alexandria, while Antioch was the center which stressed knowledge of Jesus "from below." Later scholastic distinctions would say knowledge of Christ which begins with his divinity considers his nature in the order of being—in the order of its own existence in its own right; Christology, on the other hand, which begins with Christ's humanity gives priority to the order of time—that is, to the order in which we get to know Jesus, rather than Jesus' nature considered just in itself.

Since it takes time to know a person (because, as we shall see, there is a sense in which a human person is time), we will meet Jesus "from below" in these pages. That is the way Jesus' first disciples came to know him as they lived their daily lives with him. In addition, there is little profit these days in introducing Jesus to others by title, even by such traditional titles as Messiah, Christ, and Savior, for the titles prove nothing to anyone; they only show what Jesus has been called in the past. They carry no proof of their validity and offer few clues to their original significance for those living in today's world.

A personal relation with the living Jesus is both the source and goal of Christian living. Titles, even those attributed to Jesus, have to be penetrated by our personal experience to be either meaningful or helpful to us.

Because of the personal relations and the personal experience of those who lived with Jesus, over a period of time, and especially after the resurrection, those who were closest to him became convinced that God was so completely present in Jesus' life that Jesus somehow had to be God. Nothing less could be said about him and justify the experience they had of him. Thus it was that after a time and in time Jesus was confessed by the community of those who believed in him to be truly human and truly God, true God and true man, as the Creed says.

The faith of the community having made that profession, since Jesus truly was God and human, many of those who already knew Jesus began to emphasize his deity when they carried news about him to those who had not known him. Since Jesus, according to faith, is both human and divine, the emphasis on his divine nature was legitimate. To emphasize one or the other of the aspects of his being might even appear to be purely arbitrary under the circumstances; either one would do, for both were true.

A good case can be made for first emphasizing Jesus' divine nature over his human nature when introducing him to others. It was the difference found in Jesus' life from the lives of those around him—and the difference he made in the lives of those who knew him—that made people want to tell others about him. There was something new about him that attracted others and that enabled him to bring newness to those he helped; the difference in Jesus' life was the presence of God people began to recognize in it. The newness Jesus brought to those who knew him is the reason his friends and disciples told others about him. That God had newly identified himself with human life in Jesus was the good news of the gospel. So, more and more, the deity of the incarnate Lord was stressed by those who accepted Jesus as God's revelation of himself and proclaimed him to others as the one uniquely filled with the Spirit of God.

As reasonable as the emphasis we have just described is, a consequence of it has caused, and continues to cause, considerable difficulty for those who call themselves Christians. By first emphasizing the deity of Christ, God, the Person we understand least, becomes the means of understanding Jesus, the human being with whom we have the most in common—the one we should understand best.

Going from Jesus' divinity to his humanity tends to make everything Jesus said and did (as we know about them through others) an act of God. What are taken as his remarks and his actions, as reported to us, assume the status of divine laws. Thus the deposit of faith, from which the faithful are not to depart (Jude 3), tends to be taken as a static, formal body of prescriptions from which there is no appeal. Because of the certainty with which God is taken to have spoken in Jesus, Paul's understanding of the new covenant as a gift of the Spirit of life, rather than a written code, is undermined. (Cf., II Cor. 3:6) What some see as no more than the human condition of Jesus' life, others see as divine decrees.

Within the emphasis on Christ's divinity we are describing, God made what Jesus said important, and what Jesus said made God clear. It is quite simple. The simplicity is God's gift to us. The clarity of Jesus is the certainty of God. The voice from the cloud on the mount of the transfiguration resolves all conflict: "This is my beloved Son; listen to him." (Mk. 9:7)

As much as we might wish, in our wearier moments, that such simple clarity is furnished for Christians in Jesus, another passage from Scripture comes to mind that gives us pause. The First Letter to Timothy states that "great indeed, we confess, is the mystery of our religion: who was manifested in the flesh. . . ." (3:16) We are here clearly told that clear knowledge of Jesus is limited. Jesus is a mystery. The Word made flesh is not a book; the Word is a Person, the Person of God. God is the absolute mystery of all existence. No one can understand God clearly: that, too, is Scripture.

Tension and ambiguity are found in the life of Jesus which can be neither resolved nor ignored. Human life is always lived within a horizon of ambiguity, as it has been put, or it is not truly human. Every human being is located in a given time and place in history; because of that fact, because our lives are centered in our bodies, our views of the world are always perspectives on the world. To some extent we necessarily see the world differently from each other, for we all stand in different places. No one can escape the limitations of his or her location in trying to understand reality as a whole.

We often do not clearly know what we should do now or what will happen later. We wonder about our real motives in an action, let alone the motives of other people; we can deceive ourselves as well as be deceived by others. What am I really like, we wonder. We puzzle about which principle to follow in a complicated ethical decision: do I remain scrupulously honest with the money given to me to keep, or do I secretly borrow from it to help Jerry avoid foreclosure on his house?

The human condition nurtures life that is, in many ways, not clear. We change, grow, and learn. Jesus, too, grew and learned or he would not be human. (Lk. 2:52) We read that he was not immune to temptation, a condition which requires alternative possibilities of action not automatically predetermined. (Mk. 1:13; Matt. 4:1; Lk. 4:2)

The fact of Jesus' temptation calls attention to another ambiguity in his life, an ambiguity that goes beyond the ambiguity describing human life in general. Here the lack of clarity involves the relation of Jesus' humanity to his divinity. How could Jesus be, at one time, truly God and truly human? How could he, as true God and true man, be tempted? Would his oneness with God allow him to sin? How is Christ's deity related to his humanity?

If we begin our acquaintance with Jesus from the point of view of his divinity, the genuineness of his humanity may easily be compromised. The primacy of his divine nature may allow him only to appear to be human; he cannot truly be as human as we are, living precisely as we do. He has an advantage we do not, for he is divine as well as human. An early heresy, called docetism from the Greek verb "to seem," took just that view. Docetists held that Jesus, because he was the Son of God, did not really suffer and experience life in the world as you and I do; he only seemed to. The important point is that when such an explanation of Jesus' life was considered it was totally rejected by the church.

The genuineness of Jesus' humanity is the beginning of it all. The kind of life Jesus lived as a human being was precisely what led others to recognize God in him. The presence of God in Jesus' life led none of his disciples to conclude that he was not truly human in the first place. There is not a single instance in the New Testament in which Jesus refers to himself as God or as the Son of God; his most characteristic reference to himself is to the Son of Man, a reference stressing his full participation in the human condition.

The burden of all the post-resurrection appearances of Jesus is to show that it is the very human Jesus who was one with his friends and family, who lived the same life they lived, who talked with them and told them parables, who ate and slept with them, who rose from the dead. Jesus, as you and I, was born of a human mother; he grew up and was reared in the political and religious world of his day; he was misunderstood by his friends (Mk. 3:21), attacked by his enemies, and he finally died the very

death we will die. That his life did not end in death did not destroy the genuineness of his humanity; it showed, instead, the
love of God for precisely the kind of people we are.

There is a difference between meeting Jesus in the first place
and accepting him as our Savior in the second place. Before we
can accept Jesus as our Savior, we must, as we said, meet the
right Jesus the right way. The truth of that fact, however, does
not deny that different people have different ideas about who the
"right" Jesus is and how he should be met. I shall try to present
the Jesus I know, and the reader will have to decide whether or
not that Jesus speaks to him or her. The point beyond dispute is
that before we can accept Jesus as Savior in any significant sense
we must have some personal acquaintance with him.

It is our contention that the way Jesus is introduced by those
who claim to know him may be the very thing that keeps others
from knowing him as he really is. There are those who invoke
Jesus as Savior with embarrassing naivete, for example, equating
him with the Bible they hold in their hand. For some, the Jesus
presented is so judgmental that the followers' need for acceptance and security shouts more loudly than Jesus speaks as the
Word of God. The Savior becomes no more than a zealot's echo.
For others, though Jesus is proclaimed to be risen from the dead,
he seems more accurately to be buried in the past. Such people
cannot stand the complexity of contemporary living and, in the
name of Jesus, try to return to the past, to earlier, less complicated times, denying the reality of the world in which they live.
Their Jesus does not overcome the world; he ignores it. The only
peace he can offer is through escape. In all of these instances
Jesus is used to save something, but it can be questioned whether
or not he is redeemer as well as savior; his saving seems to be
more a prolonging of some status quo than a making all things—
including his disciples—new.

First to introduce someone to Jesus as Savior is, in our view,
the wrong thing to attempt. "Savior" is a term summarizing personal knowledge; it is not a general title that one must buy into
in order first to meet Jesus. Even those who, because of the diffi-

culties they experience in their lives, are prepared to admit, as a first step, their need of a savior, may not recognize the Savior who comes. They may know only their needs—projecting what is a solution for them onto Jesus and then recommending that Jesus, their Jesus, to others.

I can significantly call Jesus "Savior" only after I have met and gotten to know him, not as a means of my first meeting him. As my Savior, Jesus engages me in a manner that carries me beyond myself—but I must first be engaged with him, and he must be the kind of person with whom I can be engaged in the daily world in which I live.

As we have indicated, we must meet Jesus in the first place before we can call him Savior in the second place. A book which truly introduced Jesus to us could well have one title in the beginning and a different title in the end—because of our meeting him. Jesus is a person, not a theory. He confronts us and calls us beyond ourselves. He is the man from Nazareth in the beginning, but we may recognize him to be our Savior in the end.

Jesus may not be the one we are most ourselves with when we first meet him, yet there is a "fit" in our knowing him, for he is with us where we are for what we are. We must not deny the possibility that one of our major difficulties may be that we do not know where we are and what we are as well as we think we do. Jesus is a Savior who comes to call us. God loves us before we love him; he doesn't wait for us to find him. That is why Jesus as our Savior breeds patience: he takes care of us, not we him.

If Jesus is inaccessible to us, because of his irrelevance to the world in which we live or because of his distance in time from us, the title "Savior" will be a stumbling block for us rather than a help to us. To see whether or not the Jesus who lived in his day can engage us today is the purpose of this book. We will try to meet and know the Jesus we believe those who became his disciples met and knew, and we shall go on to see whether that person is the one whom we, as they, can meaningfully accept as Savior.

2.

Today

Many find it difficult to be religious today. Christianity remains a scandal, just as it was in biblical times. If what Christian faith claims to have happened in the New Testament accounts happened then, it happens now; on the other hand, if it does not happen now, it did not happen then.

It is difficult being religious today; there just isn't time for it. That does not mean an increasing number of people do not have an increasing amount of time to do what they want; it means that religion cannot meet the competition for the use of our time. At least in what we call the Western World, religion is something it is hard to find time for rather than something that commands time and directs its use.

Formal religion, that is, historically conditioned, traditional religion, often seems to mean nothing in today's world. A young woman in a London bookstore, holding a book in her hand, asked a clerk what the title meant. "Creed" was in the title, and the clerk, having failed to help explain the word by its Latin root, said, "You know, it's what you say in church; it's a statement of your belief." The woman was still not helped; she had no idea what people do in church.

Even going to church and saying the Creed does not solve the problem of being religious in our day. The repetition of traditional phrases and statements frequently seems unable to help people who do go to church. If religion is in one's background, adult participation in public worship may offer a degree of stability in difficult times—it is something to fall back on for location in a world of constant change—but, again we may ask, is the religious identity so manifested strong enough creatively to direct and command the use of time in the world in which we live?

The most critical religious problem today is not direct opposition to religion but religion's irrelevance to what is going on around us. The relevance of their religion poses a question even for believers as they take part in the activities of the world in which they live, and as they try to give orientation to their lives by means of the old formulas. Even though religion may be helpful for getting through a trying day, the believer who uses religion only as a means of preventing himself or herself from falling apart knows that the religion being practiced is being sold short in its very use. God does not exist to help us get through another day; if God is God, he is the source of the universe and has something cosmic in mind in his presence with us. If we have to retreat from the world, or from the present state of the world, in order to get help from our religion, in the midst of the help we get we know we are dealing with something less than the truth we need.

From time to time I have found myself involved with group activities in which persons present were asked to tell what major event or crisis led them to discover God in their lives in a new way. I greatly dislike such exercises, because my life with God does not lend itself to such questioning. I seem to be in a constant crisis with God. I have gone to church and tried to be a practicing Christian my whole life long, and, although I believe I have experienced the presence of God in my life a number of times, that presence has never eliminated problems about God for me. As a matter of fact, the presence has, in its way, caused and intensified problems as I profess faith in God and at the same time witness events in the world that seem to contradict the presence of the God I know.

Christianity has always been a scandal—a scandal, although for different reasons, both to those who believe and to those who do not believe. In Christianity at its best, that God should love such people as we with the love manifested in Jesus, is nothing short of scandalous. At least if we are honest with ourselves about ourselves, God's love for us in Christ is scandalous. Christianity, if looked at from the point of view of reason alone, can only be called a scandal. Christianity is not a philosophical system abstracted from nature and proven deductively. Christianity is a revealed religion, and if the claimed historic events upon which it is based did not happen, nothing is left. If their historic claims are false, Christians are the most to be pitied of all people, as Paul wrote to the Corinthians. (I Cor. 15:17ff.)

Because of the extended length of many of the treatises and the impressions made by volumes upon volumes of theological books—frequently by the same author—it is often unknown and totally unsuspected that classical Western theology, as illustrated by Thomas Aquinas, for example, never claimed that reason alone could show that Christianity was even possible in a positive sense. The best that reason can do, in the Thomistic tradition, is show that what Christianity claims to have happened and believes to be true is not impossible by contradicting itself or contradicting reality as we understand it. If Christianity is true, it is true only because it happened; it did not happen because we could know it to be true before it happened.

Professing faith in Jesus as the Christ creates problems in the world as well as solving problems. Can an omnipotent God, who is love himself and who can raise someone from the dead as Jesus was raised, allow an earthquake to claim fifty thousand lives, innocent children still in the womb to be infected with HIV, and hundreds of thousands of people to starve to death in Africa while other people feed gluttonously in Europe and North America?

We may also wonder whether or not there is room for the old religion in the new world we discern today. Our understanding of the universe is very different from that of biblical times. We live in a period of clashing worlds—the worlds of science, religion, politics, business, medicine, entertainment—and we cannot simply choose the world in which we want to live and close the others out. One of the other worlds may destroy us. The threat does not come from science alone and nuclear weapons: entertainment, business, politics—even religion—can be destructive. A religion worth its name must help us live with all reality or its god is too small to be of any use in the restricted world of our choice. We are born into a world—a universe—where something big is going on, and our God must be big enough to be the beginning and end of it all, as well as being present in the middle of things.

As I continue to believe, continue to experience God in my life, and continue to confront problems in my life of faith in the world, I continue to try to understand the reasonableness of the faith by which I live. We all live in time. Time never stands still, and who has not had cause—perhaps a number of times—to shake his or her head and exclaim how different things are in "these changing times"? Can a man named Jesus, who lived two thousand years ago in a minor country on the eastern shore of the Mediterranean Sea, have any major significance for our lives in the world today? I believe he can, if he is the Jesus who is also called the Christ. But if Christ's life does have significance for us, it will be because the way he lived time in his times helps us live time in our times. What such help is and how it is made available to us will be of central concern in these pages.

Christianity arises from something that is claimed to have happened in Palestine almost two thousand years ago. As we have put it, if Christianity is true, it is true because it happened; it did not happen because we could know it to be true. Just as significantly, we must add that if what Christianity claims to have happened then did happen, it happens now, and, if it does not happen now, it did not happen then.

Time will tell.

3.

Beginnings

There is an absolute dependence of Christianity on the person, Jesus of Nazareth. Through the centuries, abstract statements about Jesus have tended to replace the living person in the concreteness of his life and times. The scandal of Christianity is that if we miss the fullness of Jesus' human life, we miss God.

Every beginning is simple; something is presented to us and we receive it. In the beginning we are all children. As we grow older and our experience widens, what was at first simply accepted as a fact often appears to be the mark of earlier naivete. Childish acceptance gives way to adult scrutiny. We weigh, ponder, analyze, and consider the world around us.

But our end is not so different from our beginning; it has a simplicity also. In the end there are things we must simply accept; our goal in maturity is to be able to accept them without being naive about them.

What we have just said about life in general can be said in a special way about Christianity. Amidst all the conflict and turmoil associated with the beginning of the Christian movement, there was a simplicity of dependence of the whole movement on one person, Jesus of Nazareth. Christianity began as a response to a specific person, and it can never outgrow its total dependence on the life of that historical figure. Jesus was totally operative as a person, at one time different from but not superior to everyone else, among the people he influenced. He attracted people to him by his mysterious life and manner, but that same life and manner disappointed and maddened others.

As Jesus' personal influence spread, he was "universalized," i.e., he was seen to be relevant to different times and situations than those in which he immediately lived. To say that Jesus' life was *seen* to be relevant to the lives of different people in different places under different circumstances is to say that his life was *interpreted* by those who had been influenced by him to be relevant to the different situations in which they found themselves. So it is that the four Gospels present four differently interpreted portraits of Jesus as his life and Spirit were seen relevant to the times and communities in which the Gospels were produced.

The Gospel bearing Mark's name, for example, is commonly thought to have been written in the decade of the 60s by someone associated with Peter; traditionally, it was held to have been written in Rome, but Syria or Palestine are other possible locations. The Gospel might well have been produced to encourage believers at the time of Nero's persecution of Christians. The Gospel would indicate that Jesus is present with his people in their suffering, for the portrait of Jesus which is painted is of the Son of Man who cannot be known apart from his suffering and death. Real faith is based on the real Jesus who suffered and died. Jesus' death on the cross is the reality factor of the kingdom of God; the latter will not come by words and wonders alone. The Christian life is a life of witness in the world on the world's terms, and the world fights against the kingdom. Christian victory will not come easily, but the Jesus who died and rose again is with the faithful in their trials.

The Gospel attributed to Matthew appears to have taken form some 20 years after Mark in the 80s; it assumes the previous destruction of Jerusalem by the Romans and might well have been written in Antioch. By this time, Christians had been expelled from the synagogues, and, as a consequence, lost the protection of the state as a recognized religion. Matthew's community appears to have been one of converts from both the Jews and the Gentiles. It is the only Gospel that refers to the community of believers as the church, thus indicating that the consequences of the delayed reappearance of Jesus were beginning to come into consciousness. The Gospel instructs people, at one time, in the Jewish roots of their faith and in the need to proclaim the Good News to non-Jews. Matthew emphasizes Jesus' role of bringing the kingdom into the world, the reign of God offered to all people. The Spirit of Jesus is given to his disciples to be his presence with them as they go to "make disciples of all nations." (Matt. 28:19)

Luke's Gospel most likely appeared in the late 80s by the hand of a non-Jewish companion of Paul, perhaps a doctor. The place of origin could be Greece, Rome, or Asia Minor. The book of the Acts of the Apostles is a continuation of the Gospel; both books were written primarily for Gentile believers. Luke is commonly known as the Gospel of compassion and love; in it Jesus is a humble person easily identifiable in his manner of living with other human beings, one who, filled with the Spirit, goes primarily to those who are in need. He comes to save those who are lost. (Lk. 19:10) Jesus is declared Lord by his resurrection, and, after his return to the Father, his Spirit is poured out on all people. In this portrait, Jesus is the gentle Savior who receives all who are in need and who continues his work through his disciples by the gift of his Spirit.

Almost everyone accepts John's Gospel as the latest, dating somewhere from 85-100 C.E., and written in Ephesus or Antioch. The community from which it came appears to have been a self-segregated one somewhat removed from the life of other Christian communities. The Gospel has a different chronology of events concerning Jesus' visits to Jerusalem than the other three Gospels, and the day of the crucifixion is different, too. In addition, it has a much more highly developed Christology. The Jesus presented here is most obviously a theologically interpreted Jesus. Jesus is the enfleshment of the eternal Word of God; as Word he pre-exists and his being is nothing less than the "I am" of God himself. Jesus is sent by the Father to bring a new commandment of love to the world, a commandment which can be carried out only by a participation in the eternal love of the Father for the Son. Jesus comes to invite us into that love; union and communion with God and each other are the marks of people who have faith in Jesus.

As the time and place of first-century Galilee and Jerusalem receded further and further into the distance, the universalization of Jesus' life by reflective interpretation on it tended to become dominant. Abstract interpretations of the meaning of Jesus' life could be most easily shared across expanses of space and time, and, in addition, human inquisitiveness and reflection posed a continuing series of questions about the man whose life started it all. An historical person is so located in time and culture that he or she may seem to be trapped there. Questions of validity for other times and places arise.

A universalized Jesus, on the other hand, is always in danger of losing the limitations and concreteness of his actual existence; he loses his identification with our lives in the world today. Jesus lived, but he often seemed to live only as a theory in theories about him, rather than in the actual world. Abstract intellectual structures replaced the flesh and blood of the historical man from Nazareth. Elaborations of the life of Jesus, which started out as helpful aids in knowing the historical person, turned into threatening rivals as time went on. It would not be too much to say that the theological Christ began to outdistance the Galilean Jesus.

The separation of the theological Christ from the Jesus who sweated and thirsted walking in the heat of Galilee has been a constant danger in the history of Christianity. Perhaps the first implicit awareness of the danger of such a separation, and the first attempt to overcome it, are found in the New Testament itself, especially in Paul, where reference to Jesus is made as "Jesus Christ," rather than just "Jesus" or "Christ" alone. In this manner, "Christ," the title, is used in conjunction with "Jesus," the man, to indicate that each is the other. After such association, the title, "Christ," the anointed one, began to be used almost as a proper name for Jesus; there were times when it was used that way. But would it be too much to say that nowadays the title, "Christ," has been so institutionalized and codified that the living Jesus often seems lost? People who keep the primacy of Jesus in their lives appear to be naive if not embarrassing. The eyes of a listener rolling towards the ceiling at the mention of Jesus' name offers a better accepted response to the name today than awe at his mystery.

Does the simplicity of Christian beginnings in the life of Jesus still have value today? The first Christians became Jesus' disciples because they saw the power of God in his life. They were convinced, by their own experience of the friend they knew, that God's power had raised Jesus from the dead and that Jesus, living after death with the Father, gives his Spirit to those who trust in him. Is such simple faith operative today? Is it lost? Is it possible?

If the simplicity of the earliest absolute dependence on Jesus is lost, what does the theological structure which sprang from it through the centuries mean? Could the later sophisticated understanding of Jesus disprove the earlier, more naive acceptance of him? Could something of lasting significance spring from a mistaken identity? All of the first disciples of Jesus thought the end of the world was near. Does that mistake invalidate the faith they placed in Jesus? Is Christianity now relativized as no more than one among a number of equally valid, or invalid, world religions? Is there anything unconditional about belief in Jesus as the Christ in which we ought to place our whole trust, withholding nothing?

As we have indicated, there was an absolute dependence of the first Christians on Jesus himself; it would not be too much to say that Christianity began as the "Jesus movement." Theological elaboration of Jesus and his life through the centuries has become so diverse and complex that the impact of the living person has frequently been lost under blankets of words. The one constant factor which has changed the least during the course of time has been the biblical record of the faith of the first Christian communities. As a result, those who advocate a "return to Jesus" often state their quest as a "return to the Bible."

The difficulty with some of the movements which advocate returning to the Bible is that they seem to end up with the Bible instead of with Jesus. The Bible offers clarity to the extent that it is printed in black and white, but many of the events it describes do not lend themselves to such clarity. In addition, there is no such thing as "the Bible." There are variant readings in different manuscripts, and there are different ways of legitimately translating the same words in the Greek texts. Any English translation of the New Testament is at least two language systems away from the actual words of Jesus.

There was a campaign in the United States a few years ago to get people to read "The Book." One can still occasionally see a car with a sticker on it saying "Read the Book." What must be realized is that "gospel," the good news, was never used as a way of referring to a book; it referred only to a proclamation, which is to say a personal testimony or communication. The Mormon religion is based on a book, but not Christianity.

A communication from one person to another, in the sense in which the gospel is such a communication, is an opening of one person's experience to another person. Personal experience is the basis of everything which has meaning in our lives, for what is totally foreign to our experience has no meaning for us. The experience of one person can help expand the experience of another by a new experience to which the second is led by the first, but without experiential contact and sharing, communication is impossible. What we call "cultures" or "civilizations" are ways of describing the experiential bonds of groups of people.

Properly taken, the Bible is the norm of the Christian experience of God, and the Bible should be read and understood in that light. The words of the Bible point beyond themselves to the people and the experiences of the people whom the words are about. That is simple enough to say, and, when so stated, no one will dispute the assertion; but when people try to use the Bible as a spiritual guide, the words sometimes seem to stand them off instead of leading them on. Descriptions of life in ancient times tend to limit the significance of events recounted to those times. It is similar to going to the theater and missing the play because of the scenery.

If the Bible conveys the good news, it must be used as a means of personal communication; it is a means of communicating the experience of God witnessed to by the first Christians. The question we must ask ourselves when reading the Bible is, "What is the experience of God of those whose witness is recounted in these pages?" What was the experience of God of those people whose lives we read about in Scripture? Their experience of God was obviously not the sentences written about them or about their experience. Sentences in a book never substitute for personal presence, nor, if their witness is correct, are lifeless sentences the only trace left of God's presence to people who lived before us. If God exists, the influence he had in the lives of people who lived before our time should also be available to us—that is, if the same God wants to be with us. The claim of Christianity is that he does. Such presence should be our concern in our Bible reading.

The first disciples of the risen Jesus proclaimed the good news of his resurrection by their personal witness and testimony, but the testimony of such witness does not stand on the word of the testifier alone. The witness of those who experienced new life in the risen Jesus was to the risen Jesus himself. Their testimony was about him and led to him. Their believability ultimately was judged by the ability of those who heard them to have the same immediate relationship with Jesus they did.

The post-resurrection situation was not unlike an event in Jesus' earlier life recounted in John's Gospel. Jesus, journeying through Samaria, stopped for a drink of water at a well near the city of Sychar. While he was resting, he spoke to a woman of Samaria, who, after her conversation with him, was so impressed that she went into the city and told people that she had met a man who so astounded her that he might be the Messiah, the Christ. She made her witness and some, we are told, believed because of her testimony. She asked the people to come and see for themselves, "and many more believed because of his word. They said to the woman, 'It is no longer because of your word that we believe, for we have heard for ourselves, and we know that this is indeed the Savior of the world.'" (Jn. 4:41f.)

The incident, although taking place before Jesus' resurrection, was written down and preserved not only after but because of his resurrection. If the resurrection of Jesus truly occurred, the significance of the event at Sychar must be as true after the resurrection as before. The only way we can be led to Jesus now is by the testimony of others, but if we cannot confirm such testimony by our own experience, the testimony will have no value for us.

The significance of the resurrection is that Jesus was raised from the dead precisely so that we could know the Father in him. It is Christian belief that God speaks so fully and uniquely to human beings in Jesus, that Jesus' personal identity will never end. That is the realization expressed in somewhat different terms in the Epistle to the Hebrews: Jesus, unlike former priests in Israel, "is able for all time to save those who draw near to God through him, since he always lives to make intercession for them." (Heb. 7:25) Jesus lives now and is available to us as the Christ. As the Christ, as the one anointed by the Spirit, the very Jesus who taught in Galilee, who was crucified and who rose again, comes to us so that, in him, we can know God as God wishes human beings to know him.

The scandal of Christianity is that, in this instance, to miss the human being is to miss God.

4.

God's Location for Us

*Those who knew Jesus best discovered such a differ-
ence in his life, that they saw nothing less than God's
inner mystery revealing itself in Jesus. Instead of knowing God only as the creator of the world, they saw, in
Jesus, God's love confronting them as another person in
the world. In Jesus, God gives himself to us in history
for history's fulfillment.*

How do you make someone who lived 2,000 years ago alive
for you?

The answer is, you don't; at least you don't if you are a Christian and the person is Jesus. Still, that is what many people try to
do and many more feel the need to do.

We can say, "Jesus lives," but the saying is not the living.
How can we receive that spark of life which would remake our
lives and which the creeds say is Jesus' continuing life?

The role of Jesus was unsubstitutable in the beginning of
Christianity. The Johannine community had such a new experience of God in Jesus that it professed the unity of Jesus with
God. Jesus was not the latest and most striking prophet; he did
not excel Moses by being in the line of prophets with Moses.
There were some who thought that to be the case during Jesus'
teaching ministry, but after the resurrection such a view was impossible for them. The disciples' experience required a choice
between Moses and Jesus. It was either one or the other; it could

not be the two together bearing the same kind of witness to God. At the time of John's Gospel, to choose Jesus was to be forced out of the synagogue; it was to lose one's family and friends. It was to stake all on Jesus.

The persecution of Christians going on at the time of Mark's Gospel, and the Gospel's response to it, further showed how the disciples of Jesus were asked to risk everything because of the gift of God they recognized in him. There was felt to be a discrete jump—a radically new beginning—with Jesus that made him first in his disciples' lives. Everything else was valuable only as it was seen in him. What God began in Jesus' life continues through the Spirit, in his name, after the resurrection. It is, for example, "by the name of Jesus Christ of Nazareth," that Peter, with John, healed the lame man at the gate of the temple. (Acts 4:10) Jesus' ministry continues because his life continues.

Still, knowing that Jesus was singularly important for the beginning of Christianity and that he was experienced alive and present with those who believed in him after his death and resurrection, does not make him spring to life for us. Just reading the Bible does not make one suddenly jump to new life in Jesus; both Jesus and the time in which he lived, and he was partially defined by his time, make knowing him difficult for people of our time. The disciples of Jesus' day had a considerable advantage.

The first Christians were Jews well established in an on-going relationship with God through Moses and the prophets, and through their understanding of God's special choice of their nation to be his people in the world. They worshipped God and lived, for better or worse, within a covenantal relationship into which they believed God had invited them. In Jesus they recognized the presence of *that* God in a new way.

Proclaiming the good news of God in Christ to the world today, the Christian message is not introduced into such a well-prepared context. Seed is not sown in such well-cultivated ground. Our situation has more in common with the problems Paul faced when he took the good news to the Gentiles, but even here differences remain. There was a more generally accepted basis of meaning then than now; there was more sharing of a common world then than we now experience. The possibilities of describing the world and what went on within it were not as varied in biblical times, even between different cultures, as they are now within what we take to be one culture.

Communication is based on sharing, and, if meaningful witness to Christian faith is to be made in today's world, it will have to be on the basis of something we, Jesus, and those who offer witness to Jesus share.

What is such shared experience? Initially it was a covenanted life with God for the Jews. Jesus offered a new covenant with the same God. The question posed by Jesus was what to do to fulfill the will of God. How does God want us to live with him? What is he saying to us about our lives? A new understanding of the nature of God developed with a new understanding of his will, but knowing God in a new way is different than knowing God for the first time. Jews who became Christians at least recognized a continuity in the background of their lives; that is why they continued to use the Old Testament and Psalms.

The question is different today. The first question produced by our cultural experience is more apt to be, "What do you mean by 'God'?" than "What does God want me to do?" "God" means different things to different people, and to some the word means nothing.

We just do not orient to reality in a manner in which God is significant. The competitive nature of our lives socially, economically, politically—at the individual, national and international levels—stresses the advantage of functional technique in order to win the game, rather than fostering the acquisition of a basic understanding of life and of the meaning of existence. The President of the United States challenges the nation's educational system to produce students second to none in mathematics and science. In his charge, the President added that students should also be able to read and communicate effectively, but being able to read and communicate in the mathematical and scientific disciplines were evidently enough. The meaning of life and the purpose of life were either totally left out of consideration or they were presumably found to be covered in mathematics and science.

The technological and economic success of other nations were the basis of the challenge the President issued to the country. The same concern about competition with others is found in our personal lives. Questions of ultimate meaning give way to our desire for competitive success; thus it should come as no surprise that people find their competitively successful lives to have no meaning.

Everything that has meaning for us has some kind of relationship to our experience. Even though we may pay no attention to it, is there not some common element of human experience which gives significance to the word "God"? If human experience is examined in its wholeness, we contend there is always found a dimension of it which is open-ended and incomplete in itself. The experience of such open-endedness offers a context for the meaningfulness of Christian claims.

To say that something is open-ended is to say that it is not complete in itself: the very nature of the thing in itself leads beyond itself. One manner in which the open-endedness of human existence manifests itself is in the many and varied religious traditions which are found in the history of the human race. The great world religions, in one way or another, are all structured by the dependence of human beings, whose individual existence is threatened, on something beyond them whose existence is not so threatened. Our total dependence on something beyond us is a structure common to all religions, although the nature of what we are dependent on varies significantly from one religion to another.

The awareness of our dependence on something beyond us, which we have suggested is the common structure of all religion, is also found in dimensions of our experience which we do not ordinarily think of as religious. It is important to recognize the structure of religious experience for what it is in itself, so we are not tied down to looking for it only in activities which are called "religious." If religious insight is to be true for anyone, it must be true for everyone—even those who do not recognize it in their lives and who profess themselves to be atheists. If the structure of which religious experience is the recognition is not a structure discernable in the existence of all human beings, religion is reduced to a psychological fantasy of some rather than offering a truth about all.

Perhaps the most basic experiential awareness of what a religious person would call the God relationship is found in the general human intuition that life is worth going on with, that living is something worth struggling to do. What accounts for the present cultural concern with physical fitness? Why are people so obsessed about good health? Why have so many eating and drinking habits changed with the health craze? People want to live longer and more fully, and they are willing to change the way they live in order to increase the amount of time they live.

Our whole scientific enterprise is based on the lived premise that there is a universe to know and that our knowledge of it makes a difference in it. Not the least difference is our ease of living. Science and technology offer us new ways in which we can exercise our wills in the world, doing what we want to the world and in the world. The unspoken premise at the basis of scientific inquiry is that reality is meaningful; in our lives we want to exploit that meaning as our self-achievement.

When we feel our lives are meaningless and we question the ultimate nature of reality, we are questioning a primal awareness of God. We learn more about the religious structure of reality when we have questions about the world's meaningfulness than when we just assume its meaning and go ahead with our specialized activities in it. Questioning every aspect of reality and our experience of it does more to lead us to the religious situation than does confining our questioning to a restricted area of reality. When our implicit awareness of God is questioned, that is, when our unrecognized assumption that life in the world has meaning and value is questioned, what has until then been tacit and unrecognized can become more explicit and recognizable. It can become directly admitted for the first time. There is stability of meaning in the world in spite of the constant flux and change of the world. If reality is reasonable, that stability needs a stable source to account for it; if reality is basically unreasonable, there cannot be even a temporary meaning assigned to the stability we recognize. To be concerned about meaninglessness at all presupposes the prior acknowledgment of meaning or else concern about lack of meaning has no significance. Why should such concern arise?

Questions about the meaningfulness of reality pose problems about the nature of God for those who believe in God by posing, for example, the question, "How can these things happen to people if God is loving and all-powerful?" Problems about the meaningfulness of reality at one time expose people to the necessity of God and question the existence of the God already acknowledged. Religion does not do away with problems; the person without problems is the only one who cannot be religious.

Even when the awareness of our dependence on God becomes more obvious to us, the experience of the dependence cannot be easily described to others. The dependence we recognize is something out of which we come, so the dependence can never be described as we describe an object in the world. The classical manner of referring to the awareness with which we are presently concerned is to say that it is the awareness of our contingency; it is the realization that we do not have to be, that by ourselves alone we are nothing. I have written about the experience on other occasions, so I will not repeat myself here. Let us just entitle the experience to which we are referring as the "other-car-coming-towards-me-in-my-lane" feeling. As the car speeds towards me and I realize there is nothing I can do, that everything is out of my control, I know myself for what I ultimately am in myself.

The structure of the experience we have just labeled can be philosophically analyzed, but the analysis is not essential to the lived awareness of the situation. In the experience itself we have an immediate awareness that if everything has the same kind of being I have, everything is absurd. Some Source beyond the kind of being I am is the only Source of the meaningfulness of my being and of the existence of the universe. That Source is called God.

The awareness of a Source from which all meaning comes offers the experiential context within which the Christian faith can have meaning for us. We have just been describing the awareness of God as the condition of meaning *for* the world; the Christian claim is that, in Jesus, God is known in the condition *of* the world.

When God is recognized as the transcendent Source of all meaning, we recognize that the whole world somehow comes from him, but we do not get any specific help about how we should live in the world in God's presence. To recognize God as the ultimate Source of reality is to recognize God, in a general way, as the ultimate Source of security, for the recognition means that existence basically makes sense and has value, but such knowledge does not lead us to risk-taking in our lives. Contemplative withdrawal from the world and its vicissitudes would be a reasonable relationship with such a God. God's presence comforts us by allowing us to escape from the world into his transcendent and nonthreatened life. That is the kind of religious peace many people seek.

To recognize God in the condition of the world is to recognize God in an historical event; it is to recognize God in a manner which could have been otherwise. To know the absolute God in an historical event which did not have to take place involves risk and trust; it is very different from knowing that God is the transcendent Source of all meaning—whatever the meaning may be. To claim a truth about God which is historical rather than eternal is to accept something as true because it happened rather than being able to argue that it happened because it is true. Mathematics works the second way; revelation works the first way.

Christians claim that God, the ultimate Source of all meaning, wants us to know him in a specific way he chooses, rather than knowing him only in a more general sense as the Source required by all being which is insufficient in itself. As creator, God underlies us; he makes us ourselves, holding us up out of nothingness, as it were, by his will. We know him through ourselves as we exist, which means we know him as the one enabling us to be what we already are. That is quite different from God confronting us as another person in the world, challenging us and questioning the life we live.

Christians believe God shows his love for us by coming to us where we are and by revealing himself within—not just beyond—the conditions of our existence. Because our being is located in a given place at a given time, God locates himself for us in a place at a time; because our fully creative personal lives require choice, commitment, and risk, so our fully creative personal lives with God involve the same ingredients. Christians take God's loving location of himself for them in space and time to be Jesus of Nazareth. Trust is involved in accepting the witness of those who claim that the life of Jesus is the revelation of God's life within the conditions of the world, but such trust is possible and meaningful because Christians see Jesus' life in the world to be God's invitation to us to know him in his internal life, rather than to know him just in his external work in creation.

Knowing God as the Source and condition of our being is to know that we are somehow *of* God; there is hope for us because our insecure being is anchored in the bedrock of God's being. But, as we said, to know God as the condition for history as a whole to take place is very different from knowing God in a specific event in history. As the condition which allows history in general to occur, God's presence tells us nothing about what our lives in history should be like. God's allowing history to occur is very different from God's directing history towards a goal; the knowledge of God's existence as the condition for history is a different kind of knowledge than the knowledge we have of actions in history. The former gives no specific direction to our lives in time, as we have said; to know God as the condition for our lives leads us to contemplation and meditation rather than stirring us to action. There are times we need to meditate and contemplate, but if such activities were the sole purpose of our lives, God's creation of the expanding energy system called the universe would seem to be excessive even for him.

It is God's love, the act of his will, that created heaven and earth; God's eternal contemplation of himself as the condition for the limitless number of things he could do produces nothing. It would be no more than a celestial day-dream. God is love; he brings creation to existence by his love, and he knows creation in his love. God did not bring the universe into existence just to allow it to be. He brought it into existence to be one kind of universe rather than another. God not only gives us the world, he gives himself to the world for the world. For the same reason that God, the condition for history, allows history actually to occur, God enters history to lead history from within to the goal he lovingly has for it. History is a flow of events. Because God is love, he never ceases to give himself: he gives himself as the condition for history by sustaining history, and then he gives himself to history in history for history's fulfillment. We know such giving in the life of Jesus.

5.

Meeting Jesus

The only Jesus we can know is the living Jesus, but too often Christians witness to a static Jesus. To confront the living Jesus, we must see Jesus in his times. Our lives are extensions of time, as is Jesus' life. In Jesus' life God gave himself a history; to be a Christian is to live time as Jesus lived it. Jesus does not remove us from time, for, when the Word became flesh, God's Truth became temporal. Because Jesus truly lived time in time he was a person of faith. Christians are not those who have a faith in Jesus; they are those who share the faith of Jesus.

Recognizing that the gospel is not a book but, instead, direct testimony by persons to events they witnessed and experienced in their lives, the New Testament leads us to a person, Jesus. In meeting Jesus, we and the biblical witness confront the ultimate mystery of reality. The foundational status of the New Testament for Christians arises from the fact that it leads us to encounter a person; the person, not the book, is the important thing.

Meeting Jesus, we do not meet a person who answers every question we have about every subject; rather, Jesus poses questions to us about the meaning of human life by the way he challenges us. Looking into the eyes of Jesus, his simple presence asks us what it means to be human. His presence also gives the answer: it is to live with God filled by God's Spirit.

That may sound fanciful or picturesque to many in the world today, but it is the life offered to us by the resurrected Jesus. And it is meaningfully offered to us in our world, as we will try to show.

Neither the sentences of Scripture nor the definitions of councils are the Word of God. The Word was made flesh, John's Gospel tells us, and it is only in meeting Jesus, the man of his day, that he can speak to us in our day. Jesus speaks to us from inside time. Entering time is how the Word became flesh, for it is by entering time that God speaks to human beings as a human being. Jesus comes to us to question us about our lives, but too frequently we are able to shut the living Jesus out of our lives by substituting sentences and definitions about him for him. By subtle means at which we are most accomplished, we are able to possess him in the guise of witnessing to him. The living Jesus becomes captive to our understanding of him and to the way we want to acknowledge him.

Do not Christians too often witness to a static Jesus, instead of a living person? Jesus is held up to the world as an institutional projection, instead of the man from Nazareth who intrigued those who listened to him and overcame his disciples by being raised from the dead. We present a Jesus who has not overcome us. Those to whom we speak in his name are quick to see that the person we are talking about has not had the strength to overcome us, so why should they believe he has the strength to overcome death? We seem to know and understand Jesus so well that when we talk about him, people meet us instead of him. Jesus becomes our possession; thus it is easily possible for us to separate ourselves from others—and from each other—and to condemn others in his name. It is difficult to bear witness to others that Jesus is Savior, when the others to whom we go do not discern his salvation in us. Jesus is Savior because he saves us from ourselves. Where do the multiplicity of Christian churches and communities come from? The one God appears to be divided up in the name of the one Son he sent. Richness and diversity are brought by the Spirit of God, but not division.

Could it be that we are afraid of the living Jesus? Could such fear be the reason we do not witness to him better? We present theories about him. Do we accept Jesus as God's love making a difference in our lives, or do we find it safer to hold Jesus at arm's length until we feel we understand what he was trying to do and then accommodate that understanding into our lives our way?

To confront the living Jesus, we must see Jesus in his times. People can know us only in our time, and until we can meet Jesus within the common temporal condition of our lives, it will be impossible to live with him. Only if we can meet Jesus within the temporal flow of our lives will it be possible for us to say with Paul that "it is no longer I who live, but Christ who lives in me." (Gal. 2:20)

Christian revelation is not a gift from God of static truths, standing outside time, separating us from time. Such a static revelation would be appropriate for a God of pure thought, who spends eternity contemplating himself, but it would not do for a God who is love. Love, as we know it, is a doing and a going, a giving and a bestowing; in our world love needs time to be itself. Accordingly, the God who is love gives himself to us in an action that takes time—and by that action God gives meaning to time for us. In our lives, loving is a way of using time.

The mystery of time has challenged the human mind through the ages; philosophers such as Aristotle, saints such as Augustine, and scientists such as Einstein have pondered its meaning. Time is not an entity in itself within which events occur, yet time measures change and orders events in the world. Human time is its full self as history; to be a person is to be a history. Most strictly speaking, a human person does not have a history; a human person is a history. We may speak of the history of a person, but a person's history cannot be separated from its owner. The historical life of a person is that person's uniqueness. What distinguishes every person from every other person in the world is the lived experience, that is, the history, of the person. We do not just live our personal lives in time; our personal lives are time. We are our past, our present, and our future; to be a person is to be a temporal extension. The ultimate way to destroy a person's life is to prevent that person from being the past, present, or future which is rightly he or she. Teen-age pregnancy, drug addiction, alcoholism, lack of education, housing that denies human dignity, poverty that enslaves, racial prejudice are all restrictions that prevent people from exercising options that should be available to them in their future so that they can become themselves. To do anything to a person which unnecessarily limits the person's future is to wound that person in the depths of his or her being; on the other hand, someone who wants to live only in the past, and who ignores the present because of preoccupation with the past, suffers self-inflicted wounds as a person.

Because God wants us to love him as a person, he makes himself a person for us by giving himself a history in Jesus. As we noted, John's Gospel tells us that the Word became flesh in Jesus, and Christian orthodoxy has elevated that statement to creedal status. It may be wondered, however, whether or not the meaning of the claim is truly understood by many who profess to anchor their faith in it. Put in other words, the statement says that God's Truth entered time in Jesus. The scandal of that statement must be made clear. When eternal Truth entered time in Jesus, the Truth did not hover above Jesus outside of time; the Truth became temporal! God's Truth is a life, not a collection of ideas; the living God could not reveal himself as a static proposition. A God of eternal contemplation might reveal himself in a timeless thought which remains unchanged in time, but he would have a bigger problem than even he might be able to manage if he tried to translate the perfection of the timeless insight into something which requires growth and change, as does human life. It would be easier to bring forth a new creation more in keeping with himself. But why would a God whose whole being is consumed in self-contemplation want to create anything beyond himself in the first place?

A God whose Truth is love, on the other hand, could not impossibly reveal something significant about his inner Life in a human life. If God is love, it is also understandable why God would want to share his life with others to such a degree that he freely creates others to have someone to share himself with. Jesus is the love which is the Father as that love can be seen.

Jesus is the Word of God as the Word is spoken in history; the life of Jesus is an event—a series of events—in the world. Speaking is an event that takes time, so when God speaks to human beings his speaking takes time. For the God who is love, time is not an imperfection to avoid; it is the means by which love's meaning is achieved.

When the Word became flesh, God himself was telling us that it is impossible to know him in fleshless concepts. Abstract knowledge is not our deepest knowledge of God. In the Word made flesh God reveals that the only way we can know him in his inner life is in the fullness of our fleshly lives in the world. Love's meaning is not a timeless definition; it is bodily action, the spending and using of time for the glory of God and the growth of others. Invisible contemplation cannot contain the fullness of love; God's love can be seen. What if God's Word in Jesus is that there is no love of him that cannot be seen? If that is the case, could all those who presently consider themselves lovers of God legitimately continue such self-regard? Everything "Christian" is lived, not "ideal." A primary temptation of the religious life is to remove ourselves from history, in the name of God, and thereby forego the need for trusting in God with a total dependence in time.

Malcolm Muggeridge entitled his autobiographical series, *Chronicles of Wasted Time.* Anthony Powell produced a 12 volume set of novels under the title, *A Dance to the Music of Time.* The series is a chronicle of the lives of four men from the time they were together in their youth at boarding school through their mature lives into the approach of old age. What to do with time, and how to express ourselves in the time of our lives, are ways of expressing the basic challenge confronting every person as a person.

Time may not be a thing in itself, as we have mentioned, but as it is marked by our clocks and calendars it does call the tune for us—so it is something to which we dance. Human life is a chronicle; thus it can be chronicled. "Chronicle" comes from the Greek word *chronos*, meaning a period of time. The hands on the clock continue to move even when we want them to stop; there are occasions in which we are so involved in what we are doing that we do not notice the passing of time, but even when we do not notice it continues to pass. There comes a time in everyone's life when he or she realizes with an earnestness only joked at before, "I am old." The pharmaceutical industry is in perpetual search for an elixir which will "reverse the aging process," but everyone knows the product being sought will be something to rub on the skin to change the appearance of time rather than something which will reverse the course of time. Injections of human growth hormone have now been discovered to firm skin in the elderly, increase muscle tissue and decrease fatty tissue; a more youthful appearance has resulted from treatment, but no increase in longevity has resulted to date. It is just that the elderly feel more robust in their old age. Our lives are constituted by the arrow of time; our future will never be our past, and our past will never be our future.

The temporal structure of our lives is so basic to us that, if the structure were removed, we would no longer be ourselves. To cease having a future and a past is to cease being human. If our lives continue after death, we will continue to be temporal after death also. It is—and it will be—impossible for us to get away from time. Successful living is learning how to live time rather than trying to escape it. "Creative living" is creative in its use of time; uncreative people try to flee time. Drugs and alcohol are attractive because they make the awareness of time disappear. A few good drinks at the beginning of a boring evening help a lot. At the other end of the scale, time can be negated by trying to escape into the transcendent in meditation. How strange it would be for God to make himself temporal for us in Jesus, if his purpose in coming to us was to take us out of the time into which he put us. An endless future rather than no future is God's gift to us in Jesus' resurrection.

To know Jesus as the Word of God spoken in history is to know him as a man of faith. God's Truth did not hover above Jesus as an unseen store of eternal knowledge to which Jesus had access during his earthly life. Jesus' human knowledge was not God's eternal knowledge, so that, knowing everything, he had a security which can never be ours. Jesus faced a future unknown to him, just as our future is unknown to us; he lived a life just like ours—a life of perspective and growth. The historical limitations of Jesus are not a defect in God's presence to us in Jesus; they are precisely what make Jesus' life liberating for us. In the classic words of Irenaeus, the great second-century Bishop of Lyons, Jesus "became what we are to enable us to become what he is." To vary the wording of the ancient insight, we may say that if Jesus did not truly come to where we are he cannot take us to where he is. It is hard to get a lift from an elevator—or a religion—that doesn't stop on your floor.

Our salvation in Jesus depends upon his having lived in the world exactly as we do. It is only because we can recognize our lives in Jesus and his life in ours that the Epistle to the Hebrews can say that we look to him as "the pioneer and perfector of our faith." (Heb. 12:2) That Jesus is the pioneer of our faith is most significant for our relationship with him. The King James translation refers to Jesus as the "author and finisher of our faith." The Greek word *archēgos,* translated either as "pioneer" or "author," comes from the word *archē,* meaning "beginning" or "origin." The force of the statement in either translation is that Jesus offers us something which, after his accomplishing it, we too can do: he makes something available to us.

What does Jesus make available to us? His faith.

The Greek text says that Jesus is the originator and perfecter of "the faith." The text does not have a possessive pronoun specifying whether the faith is Jesus' or ours, but if Jesus is the originator of something for us, the meaning must be that he is the source of something which can be ours. The plain meaning is that Jesus' faith can be our faith, and that is possible only if the faith of Jesus is what our faith is called to be. Faith must play the same role in his life it plays in ours; he did not know everything in a manner that made faith—absolute trust in God in time—unnecessary for him.

The universalization of Jesus that takes him out of his time, and the attempt to accept him as God before we receive him as a person living time, have combined to make many people feel it is an insult to Jesus to think he lived with God in the same trusting relationship we must. In order to accept Jesus as the Son of God, such people make him so different from us and give him such an advantage over us that they prevent God in his love from truly coming to us as we are. It is a case where knowledge—ours— limits love—God's.

Translation is always an interpretation and our present concern offers a splendid example of how a theological understanding brought to a text influences the translation of the text. The Revised Standard Version of Galatians 2:15-16 reads: "We ourselves, who are Jews by birth and not Gentile sinners, yet who know that a man is not justified by works of the law but through faith in Jesus Christ, even we have believed in Christ Jesus in order to be justified by faith in Christ, and not by works of the law, because by works of the law shall no one be justified." A more literal translation of the same passage reads: "We, Jews by nature and not sinners of the Gentiles, knowing that a person is not justified by works of law but through the faith of Christ Jesus, even we believed so that we might be justified by the faith of Christ and not by works of law, because by works of law, no flesh will be justified." The words translated "in Jesus Christ" in the RSV version are genitive in the Greek and would be more accurately translated "of Jesus Christ." Why was the interpretation made? We may wonder if it was because the translators thought Jesus did not or could not have faith? If he could not, or if he could but did not, what help will he be to us?

Continuing a little further along in the Epistle to the Galatians, we come to a verse of which we have already taken partial notice. The RSV reads: "I have been crucified with Christ; it is no longer I who live, but Christ who lives in me; and the life I now live in the flesh I live by faith in the Son of God, who loved me and gave himself for me." (Gal. 2:20) Once again a more literal translation would be: "I live no longer, but Christ lives in me: the life I now live in the flesh, I live in the faith of the Son of God, loving me and giving himself for me." Again the words translated "in the Son of God" are genitive and should be more literally translated "of the Son of God."

The Revelation to John, in an entirely different context, when speaking about the endurance of the saints, significantly says that they are the ones who keep God's commandments "and hold fast to the faith *of* Jesus." (Rev. 14:12. Italics mine.) In this instance the translators make the literal translation of the genitive correctly, instead of transposing its meaning as in the other instances to which we have called attention.

Writing to the Philippians, Paul speaks of being found in Christ and not having a righteousness of the law, but a righteousness "which is through faith in Christ, the righteousness from God that depends on faith." (Phil. 3:9) An alternative translation would read that the righteousness to which Paul refers is "through the faith of Christ, the righteousness from God depending on faith." The RSV translation "in Christ" is once more the genitive "of Christ." The righteousness Paul claims comes from his living the faith of Jesus, not from the more external relationship of living a faith in Jesus.

To understand Jesus as a person of faith, as someone trusting himself to God in time as we are asked to do, is the only way Paul's reference to Jesus as the "first-born among many brethren," in his Epistle to the Romans, makes sense. (Rom. 8:29) The word translated "among" also means "in." There is no doubt that Paul's understanding of Jesus here is as one who stands with those who follow him in a continuous line; Jesus is not being referred to as someone who stands above everyone else because he is different from them. In the Spirit of Christ we live time as Jesus does. Jesus is not an example of a way of living which is beyond him; he is the Way. He himself is the only Way we can successfully live our lives; that is why it is necessary for his faith to be our faith. Only if our faith becomes one with his faith can his life become our life.

6.

God's Truth as Time

Jesus does not come to test our faith; he comes to offer his faith to us. In the Spirit we live the same openness to God Jesus does. Jesus' inner disposition becomes our inner disposition, and we never have to undergo anything alone. The Spirit is given for walking, not sitting, and to walk in the Spirit is to be a follower of Jesus. Because Jesus is God-with-us, the trinitarian life of God is found within Jesus' life—not beyond it. The Trinity is not an inference from Jesus beyond Jesus; there is no Jesus to know apart from his doing the will of the Father in the Spirit.

"The faith" for a Christian is not a form of words beginning, "I believe that . . . ." It is a relation of trust. Christian faith is a trusting relationship with God we achieve by living the trust of Jesus.

In Christianity, Jesus is not so much the object of our faith as he is the source of it. Jesus does not come to test our faith; instead he comes to offer his faith to us and to make participation in his faith possible for us. The way Jesus lived the extension of time which was his life is the way we are meant to live the extension of time which is our life. Through the Spirit, the history that is our lives can be incorporated into the history that is Jesus' life. Jesus' trust in the Father becomes our trust. To believe as Jesus believed is to be open, as he is open, in his dependence.

We depend on Jesus *in* his dependence on the Father. Our faith in Jesus is to have his faith.

When we say that we are not saved by our faith in Jesus but by Jesus' faith, we mean that we are not saved by an external dependence on Jesus that can be manipulated and secured for our benefit, but by living the same inner trust and dependence on the Father that Jesus lived on earth—and now lives in glory.

It is through our sharing in the Spirit that our lives are incorporated into Jesus' life. When we receive the Spirit we receive, as a gift, the hidden depth and disposition of Jesus' life; in the Spirit we are taken into the intimacy of Jesus' relationship with the Father. The gift of the Spirit is not a magical bestowal of power that will make our lives easy or effortless. Jesus does not give the Spirit to us so that we can have God's power to make us feel secure while we remain the way we are; Jesus gives the Spirit to us so that we can live as extensions of his life without fear for our lives. Freed from concern about ourselves, we are available to do the will of God as Jesus does.

When we earlier spoke about the presence of the resurrected Jesus in our lives, we said that, if Jesus lives in glory, we today should be able to experience his presence in a manner not unlike that in which the people of Sychar directly experienced Jesus for themselves when they came to meet him, rather than having to depend only on the words of the woman who first talked to Jesus at the well. No doubt we learn about Jesus from others, but we must experience his presence in our lives for ourselves if our religion is to be anything more than empty words repeated from the past. Let us, then, take a minute to describe what the experience of the risen, glorified Jesus in our lives is like.

We said earlier there is a difference between the awareness we subtly feel, in the intuition of our own threatened being, of God's presence as the being that knows no threat and of our awareness of God confronting us one place rather than another in the world, in Jesus. The first mode of God's presence is recognized in our awareness of the being we already are; the second mode is a call to become more than we already are.

As we can know Jesus today, he is, at one time, that presence of God within us which cannot be lost, and a call beyond us to live his faith—that is, his openness—to the Father in the world.

The first mode of recognizing God's presence might be called "generic" in the sense that it is an awareness open to everyone of an ultimate reality within which we find ourselves; it is an encounter open to Jews, Muslims, Hindus, and to any number of additional persuasions, as well as to Christians. The second mode of recognizing God's presence is peculiarly Christian; it is the recognition that Jesus is Lord and Messiah.

The liberating experience of Christians is the discovery that the two modes of God's presence we have just described are found in each other: the certitude of meaningfulness in general is known in its fullest expression in the life of Jesus. The uniquely Christian experience of God's presence is to know the assurance God gives to reality as a whole in the life of Jesus—resurrected. To discover in Jesus, at one time, the stability all threatened being requires if it is to be saved from absurdity, and the free choice all human beings are called to make in response to God's love, is the experiential content in Christian life of the verbal confession that Jesus Christ is "true God and true man."

In summary we may say that the Christian experience of Jesus as the Christ is the deep feeling that life/reality is meaningful, on the one hand, and the acceptance of Jesus as the fullest human expression of that meaning, on the other hand. Our experience of the risen Jesus is our experience of the lasting meaningfulness of human life in God; it is our experience of the certitude that God loves us.

The gift of the Spirit is the gift of Jesus' inner self in our lives so that his disposition becomes our disposition. We never have to undergo anything by ourselves alone. No matter what comes, how strange or new it may be, he leads us into it. We follow him. Such following is an act of intimacy, not a mark of distance or external imitation.

Because Jesus is the pioneer of our faith, he is our companion in faith. Jesus comes to be with us, leading us to the Father; Jesus is the Way to the Father, not a replacement for the Father. Instead of being a replacement, Jesus is the Father's presence to us, for Jesus is the Father's love speaking to us as the source of our knowledge and love of the Father. "He who has seen me has seen the Father," Jesus tells Philip in John's Gospel. (Jn. 14:9) Matthew's community accepted Jesus in these words: "All things have been delivered to me by my Father; and no one knows the Son except the Father, and no one knows the Father except the Son and any one to whom the Son chooses to reveal him." (Matt. 12:27)

Because of their experience of Jesus and of his presence with them after his death and resurrection, the first Christians accepted a mysterious identity of Jesus with God. Only in that way could God make himself available to human beings by giving himself a history which could be shared with them. The strength of early Christian witness to the oneness of Jesus with God is found in the biblical record, but, once again, some translations hide the fact rather than revealing it. The "I am" passages in the Gospel of John bear record to the witness of which we are speaking, but Mark's Gospel offers corroboration also.

One of the most important Old Testament texts used in classical Western theology for explicating Jesus' relationship with God is found in the Book of the Exodus, where Moses' encounter with God in the burning bush is described. God tells Moses that he wants him to lead the people of Israel out of Egypt and:

> Moses said to God, "If I come to the people of Israel and say to them, 'The God of your fathers sent me to you,' and they ask me, 'What is his name?' what shall I say to them?" God said to Moses, "I AM WHO I AM." And he said, "Say this to the people of Israel, 'I AM has sent me to you.'" (Ex. 3:13f.)

More recent biblical studies have indicated that the name of God given Moses could be translated, "I AM WHAT I AM," or,

"I WILL BE WHAT I WILL BE," as well as simply "I AM."
(The alternate translations are noted in the RSV.) The Scholastics
took the name to mean that God is Being itself; God is Being
which must be. Because God is Being itself, all of the perfections
we find in partial beings are found perfectly in him. The first
thing to be known about God, accordingly, is his existence; from
that existence all his perfections flow.

There is continuing debate about how the Hebrew name
YHWH, which is usually rendered in English as Yahweh, should
be translated. Whatever the final decision may be, there is no
doubt that the name refers to God's unique being. Thus, when the
words I AM were seen or heard by Jews of Jesus' day, their first
association would be with God's way of referring to himself in
their tradition.

With that background, we once more find a translation that is
not as helpful as it might be when Jesus, sitting with Peter and
James and John and Andrew on the Mount of Olives across from
the temple, warns his disciples to beware of pretenders who will
come in his name to lead them astray by saying, "I am he!" (Mk.
13:3-6) The Greek text says the pretenders coming in Jesus'
name will say, "I am," not "I am he." "I am" conveys a shocking
relationship with God lacking in the RSV translation, but which
was in the mind of everyone involved in the actual event.

The full meaning of Jesus' remarks are not disguised in the
RSV translation of Jesus' conversation with those who claimed
he glorified himself by making himself greater than Abraham,
whose children the Jews were. When "Jesus said to them, 'Truly,
truly, I say to you, before Abraham was, I am,'" his hearers
would have felt that his claim of superiority to Abraham was
nothing in comparison with the blasphemy of his equating himself with God. (Jn. 8:58) Still other statements of Jesus quoted in
John's Gospel do not bear their full weight in the RSV translation. In verse 24 of the 8th chapter, Jesus says, "I told you that
you would die in your sins, for you will die in your sins unless
you believe I am he." In verse 28, Jesus is quoted as saying,
"When you have lifted up the Son of man, then you will know

that I am he, and that I do nothing on my own authority but speak thus as the Father taught me." In neither instance does the Greek text say, "I am he;" the Greek has Jesus say simply, "I am."

In Jesus' farewell discourse with his disciples before his death, recounted in the 13th chapter of John, the RSV translation quotes these words of Jesus: "I tell you this now, before it takes place, that when it does take place you may believe that I am he." (Jn. 13:19) The Greek more literally reads: "I tell you now before it happens, so that you may believe when it happens that I am." In other "I am" passages in John, Jesus does not simply say, "I am;" instead he goes on to say that he is the Way, the Truth, the Life, the resurrection, the good shepherd, the gate, and the bread of life. Even in those instances the people who heard him would think of the I AM who is God himself. Jesus is a special person because his being is discerned to be mysteriously one with God's being. Those who were led to this discernment recognized that Jesus is the only human being truly to exist. Their true existence, therefore, could be found only in him.

Living in companionship with Jesus, the disciples eventually found Jesus to be a source of new life for them. What began in him continued in his name after the resurrection through the gift of the Spirit. Time, instead of being an enemy increasingly separating him from them, became the means by which his ministry grew and spread in the world.

The gift of the Spirit makes our lives truly temporal, that is, life in the Spirit makes time become the means of our fulfillment—the means of our being what we are called to be—rather than the means of our destruction. If one spends time sitting in front of a mirror watching the advance of age written in the creases of the skin, time is an enemy we all fight and to whom we all eventually surrender. But the gift of the Spirit is not something we sit around with waiting for time to run its course; the Spirit is given for quite a different purpose.

Paul wrote to the Galatians, "If we live by the Spirit, let us also walk by the Spirit." (Gal. 5:25) A little earlier Paul exhorted the Galatians to "walk by the Spirit." (Gal. 5:16) The Spirit is for walking; there is a difference between "living" and "walking." Paul is saying that the Christian life is not one of bare existence; it is not a sedentary life, one in which we sit looking at ourselves and praying that God will make things better. To walk in the Spirit is to be a follower of Jesus Christ, the one anointed in the Spirit. The gift of the Spirit is itself only in its use; we do not receive the Spirit before we walk in it, for the presence of the Spirit is always known in some kind of movement. The Spirit has been compared to a wind blowing where it will, and wherever the wind blows things are stirred up and moved about. Walking in the Spirit indicates our acceptance of the gift we have been offered; not to walk in the Spirit is the way we refuse God's gift.

Jesus' disciples are walkers because, filled with the Spirit, they follow Jesus. A disciple is someone who learns from another and then follows the person who is the teacher. Pupils literally followed their teachers from town to town and from place to place in the ancient world. The influence of a teacher then, as now, was known by his following, but "following" was taken more literally then than now.

Because the Word became flesh, we cannot know the Father "in Christ" merely by contemplating our spiritual presence in Jesus; we can only know the Father by actively following Jesus, which is to say, by becoming his disciples. To know God "in Christ" does not mean to try to get inside of Christ in a psychological or imagined sense; it means, instead, to know the Father by following Jesus. Jesus is God's Word calling us to the Father; hearing his call, we follow him. Christian discipleship is the acknowledgment that Jesus is our unique teacher; because he is God's Truth incarnate, we follow him.

In John's Gospel, Jesus says that the Spirit will lead us into all truth (Jn. 16:13), and life in the Spirit, we have just seen, is described as a walking. Putting the two insights together leads us to the recognition that Christian truth is something to do rather than just think about. That is exactly what we would expect, if God's Truth is love, because, for love, meaning is a doing. Christians, because they love, must do the truth, not just contemplate it. Using the King James translation because of its closeness to the Greek, we read: "If we say that we have fellowship with him [God], and walk in darkness, we lie, and *do* not the truth: But if we walk in the light, as he is in the light, we have fellowship one with another, and the blood of Jesus Christ his Son cleanseth us from all sin." (Cf. I Jn. 1:6f. Italics mine.) Christian truth is something we do by following Jesus; the Christian life is itself only in the walking.

As Jesus walked in the Spirit, the temporal reality of his life, and so the oneness of his faith with ours in time, is shown beyond doubt in Jesus' cry from the cross, "My God, my God, why hast thou forsaken me?" (Matt. 27:46) The anguish of the cry poignantly shows that Jesus had more than a conceptual relation with the Father; Jesus had a living relationship with the Father that required time to be itself. A timeless concept of God cannot forsake anyone—and for the same reason a relationship with God that is purely conceptual cannot help anyone, as so many people know who think about religion but get no help from their thoughts. Jesus lived his faith in time precisely as we are called to do; the future was truly future to him, and his trust in the Father was the only specific knowledge he had of the future.

We have talked about knowing the Father through the Son. We have talked about the Father sending the Son, and we have said that to be a disciple of Jesus is to walk in the Spirit as Jesus did. Christian faith accepts Jesus as the Spirit-filled Son of God doing the will of the Father in the world. So it is that the life of Jesus led the church to its most intimate discernment of God's interior life—to the distinguishing heart of the Christian faith, the doctrine of the Trinity. We are immediately led into God's inner life by the life of Jesus.

God's presence was experienced so directly in Jesus' life by those who bore witness to him as the Messiah that they could only accept him as uniquely begotten of the Father and inspired by the Father. The immediacy of God's presence in Jesus' life led those who knew him to assert that somehow the distinguishable aspects of Jesus' life were dimensions of the inner life of

God himself. The life of Jesus was for them nothing less than the key to the life of God. Jesus came from the Father and was inspired by the Father. Compelled by their experience of Jesus, Christian believers could do no better than describe the life of the God they saw in Jesus' life as involving the interpersonal relations of a Father eternally generating a Son and just as eternally inspiring the Son with the gift of his Spirit.

Jesus is himself only as the Son of the Father in the Spirit. When any one Person of the Trinity is known, that Person is known as already related to the other two Persons. The Persons of the Trinity do not first exist as isolated individuals and then become related at a later time; each Person is nothing apart from his relation with the other two Persons.

We do not—and we cannot—get to know Jesus by degrees: when we know *him* we are already related to the Father in the Spirit, for he is nothing apart from his relation to the Father and the Spirit. When Paul said that no one could call Jesus "Lord" except by the Spirit, he did not mean that we must first know the Spirit and later call Jesus "Lord"; he meant that knowing Jesus as Lord is the knowing of the Spirit. Jesus and the Spirit are known in each other. The experience of God coming all at once explains the suddenness and the newness, the surprise and the victory, that always characterize God's revelation of himself. The wholeness of God is God's gift to us; we never know God by adding parts.

There is no temporal sequence in the relation of the Persons of the Trinity to each other; the inspired obedience of Jesus to the Father is itself a whole in which the Father, Son, and Holy Spirit are interrelated. The human life of Jesus is the reason why, in the terms of classical trinitarian theology, the Son is said eternally to proceed from the Father by the mode of "generation" and the Spirit just as eternally by the mode of "spiration," that is, by the mode of breathing or inspiration.

The words and images we use to describe God's inner life are inadequate, to be sure. Coming to us in his love and making himself temporal for us in Jesus, we know God in the begetting and inspiring of Jesus; but God does not live his interior life in time as we do, thus when we try to describe God's life as a begetting and a giving (or inspiring) we know our knowledge does not count for much. Beware of theologians who can write long books about God's interior life! But words which are inadequate for clear knowledge, when lived as Jesus lived them, can be God's gift of unending life to us because they are the gift of God's life itself. The simple fact is that God, in his love, gives us more than we can understand. He gives us himself!

7.

To Accept or Not to Accept

The Christian life is not an attempt to put a theory into practice; it is the incorporation of our lives into a life already going on in the world. If I do not accept Jesus as my Savior, the statement that Jesus is the Savior of the world has no meaning. Looking at the big picture is a way of keeping ourselves out of the picture. The kingdom of God exists in the actions and relations of human beings with each other and the world. The kingdom of God exists in our personal lives; it is not a place in itself waiting for us to move in.

Christian faith is a life of response to Jesus, we have said; it is not the holding and practicing of a list of beliefs or rules. To live the life we are describing, we have to meet a Jesus who engages us and lives convincingly enough in the same world we do to enable us to share his faith. The Christian life depends upon relating to Jesus as a living person, not just as a symbol.

We have also said that faith is not so much an openness to God in a moment of contemplation, which negates the awareness of time, as it is a manner of living time. Similarly, the Christian life does not consist in trying to actualize an ideal in the world; it rather consists of being incorporated into an action already going on in the world. To say that Jesus is the pioneer of our faith is to say that we do not start something anew or try something as an experiment in his name; we are incorporated into what began—

and continues—in his life. In the Spirit we are taken up into something already going on independently of us but open to us.

Everything we have been saying depends upon one thing, the presence of the living Jesus to us. Writing to the Philippians, Paul told them to be anxious about nothing, because "the Lord is at hand." (Phil. 4:5f.) In the Greek text, Paul says that the Lord is "near," and there is little doubt that the nearness to which Paul referred was the anticipated second coming of Jesus in glory. By the time Matthew's Gospel was written, decades after the Epistle to the Philippians, Jesus had still not returned in the manner in which the first disciples thought he would, but the delay did not mean Jesus was absent from his disciples. Matthew's Gospel ends with the resurrected Jesus saying, "I am with you always, to the close of the age." (Matt. 28:20)

We must again look at the Greek text to get the full significance of the just-quoted words for our purposes. The humanness of Jesus' presence with us does not show in the usual translation of Matthew's account. The adverb "always" in the English translation is not an adverb in the Greek; it is a three-word phrase. The Greek reads: "I am with you all the days until the fulfilling of the age." The Greek indicates that Jesus will be with us day by day, in the needs and activities that vary and change from day to day; he is not with us in a manner that treats all of our time as if its individual moments and events made no difference. His presence does not remove us from the specificity of each day; he comes to us in the specificity of each day. He does not hover above us, directing our lives from a tranquil beyond.

When John says that "the Word was made flesh and dwelt among us," (Jn. 1:14) the root meaning of the word translated "dwelt" is "tabernacled" or "tented." People who tent are on the move, journeying, moving from one place to another. So it is that God's Word entered time and remains in time for us. Jesus is present with us, in the Spirit, as we drive to work; attend a funeral; ignore someone in need; feel disappointment because of a job we did not get; hope for a sunny weekend; fear lingering illness in old age; decide how much to spend on a night out; respond to institutionalized injustice and personal prejudice; experience the joy of first love; nurse a sick child; and use or abuse the natural world in which we live. God, in Jesus, did not come to be with us for a while and then abandon us, leaving us with no more than an example of his presence in a bygone age.

Within the community from which John's Gospel arose, the meaning of Jesus' last words in Matthew were understood in a manner which made it quite compatible with Paul's advice to the Philippians. For John, the glorified Jesus returned to his disciples in the giving of the Spirit after Jesus' resurrection. Shortly before his death, Jesus tells his disciples: "I will pray the Father, and he will give you another Counselor, to be with you forever, even the Spirit of truth, whom the world cannot receive because it neither sees him nor knows him; you know him, for he dwells with you, and will be in you. I will not leave you desolate; I will come to you." (Jn. 14:16-18)

In John the expected second coming of Jesus is fulfilled in the gift of the Spirit as part of the Easter event. Jesus says he will come again, and then he gives his Spirit to the disciples. John's Gospel, as the biblical witness in general, identifies the Spirit with God's glory. When Jesus was teaching in the temple and the people did not understand a metaphor he used when referring to the Spirit, we are told the inability of the listeners was due to the fact that "as yet the Spirit had not been given, because Jesus was not yet glorified." (Jn. 7:39) For John, the gift of the Spirit is the presence of the living, glorified Jesus. Jesus did not leave his disciples to struggle on without him.

Even after his death and resurrection, nothing separates Jesus and those who follow him. Only in the immediacy of his presence is it possible to participate in Jesus' life and in his relationship with the Father. Nothing gets in between Jesus' life and those who trust in him; he invites us into immediate presence with him by sharing the Spirit of his inner life with us.

We cannot produce by our effort alone the type of relationship with Jesus to which we are referring. Our relationship with Jesus is with another person, and the other person, Jesus, must present himself to us for who he is, if we are to have a relationship with him. It is the difference of Jesus' life which makes the difference in our life, and that difference is something we can receive only as a gift. The essential Christian activity in the world is witness to what God initiates in Jesus and offers us in the Spirit. Jesus invites us to come to him and to follow him; his invitation comes to us through the witness of past generations, but the invitation itself comes from Jesus, not his witnesses. A difficulty for many is how to accept the invitation Jesus offers.

No one likes to make a mistake and especially so when one's whole life is at stake in a decision. Jesus invites us to share in the history which is his life, and we know about his life through the witness made to it. That witness is itself a manner of living, and it is by our contact with people whose lives attract us that we want to live as they do. We have to be exposed to Christian living and find it attractive before we can opt for it ourselves. But most of us would like there to be a further step we could take to get a taste of Christian living before we make a final decision about it or commitment to it. Is there not a way we can check the life out before we try it, so that we can enter it with some protection? That would be the prudent way to proceed. We would like a trial offer.

Unfortunately, there is no way to check out or test the Christian life for ourselves before we live it. The only way we can find out what accepting an invitation is like is by accepting it. Christianity is not the living out of a theory; it is a witness to something claimed to have happened by allowing the happening to happen in us. If nothing happened in the first place, in Jesus, nothing will happen in the second place—our place.

Jesus invites us into his life; actually living that life as his gift to us is the only way we can test it. Not to try living it is to avoid or ignore or refuse it rather than to test or examine or evaluate it. Commander Adam Dalgliesh, a police detective created by the mystery writer P.D. James, is a policeman who writes poetry. On one occasion, when questioning an older woman, the woman observes that it is unusual for a policeman to write poetry, and she

asks the Commander how his poetic inspiration occurs. He re-
plies by saying that a poem begins with poetry, not with an idea
for poetry. He goes on to say that poetry is an experience—and it
goes without saying, we might add, that experience can only
begin with experience. So it is with the life of Jesus. It is an
experience, not a thought. Jesus' life, if Jesus is our Savior as
Christians hold, is something we can experience; it is not a hypo-
thetical existence we can understand by just thinking about it. We
must enact it to achieve its meaning, but we enact it by accepting
the gift of Jesus' Spirit, not by trying to live it on our own.

The only way we can trust in Jesus is to trust in Jesus. The
only way to trust anyone is to live the trust. We can always quit
trusting, but we will always trust something or someone. Trust is
the only way we move into the future, even if our trust is in a
drug which makes us unaware of the future. The difficulty with
trusting is not how to get it—everyone trusts something or someone—but where to put it. A Christian puts his or her trust in
Jesus because of other people's experience of Jesus; the only way
we can know the Jesus to whom the witnesses testify is to know
him as they testify to him. We must let ourselves go and accept
him as he is presented to us, or we will keep him from being
himself and offering anything new to us.

When it is said that Jesus is our Savior, come to save us from
ourselves, the only meaning the statement can have in my experience is that Jesus is my Savior, come to save me from myself. If
I do not accept Jesus as *my* Savior, the generalized statement,
"Jesus is our Savior," has no experiential meaning for me. I may
utter the sentence, but, if so, I will literally not know what I am
saying. "Saving" is an action which can be known only in the
doing; to abstract the action from the act, as we do when we talk
about saving or merely think about it, is to be left with nothing
saving at all. If I am drowning, telling me of how I can be saved
is very different from saving me; the difference is not unlike calling Jesus "Savior" and not accepting him as my Savior. The attempt to know Jesus as Savior before trusting him as my Savior,
which appears to be the sophisticated thing to do, is actually the

most naive mistake that can be made. There is a difference between our words and our lives. God's Word in Jesus is a life that
speaks not just to our ears but to our lives, or we do not hear him
at all. Life speaks only to life.

Perhaps we are not so naive after all. The real God always
makes a difference in our lives. May that not be the reason we do
all we can to keep from recognizing him there—and best of all if
we can do so in his name? God, we say, is creator of heaven and
earth: if we can escape from ourselves to the heavens or somewhere else on earth we will have an easier time of it. We can
keep ourselves from facing God and, at the same time, we can
pretend to be fearless and objective, for we can say we are set-
tling for nothing less than "the big picture." We consider God in
relation to everything.

The advantage we gain by holding the big picture is that it is
we who take the picture, and in taking it we leave ourselves out.
We do not want our picture taken; we want to stand beyond what
could be revealed about us to us. We do not want to see ourselves in God's presence. People who are afraid they won't look
good always try to avoid the camera; they never want to be in-
cluded in the picture. So it is with us. In the appearance of being
objective and selfless, the approach *we* wish to take, *our* subjective preference prevails, and we save ourselves from becoming
aware of the only God who could be God—the God who saves
us.

We know Jesus through the testimony and witness of others,
but Jesus' own life was a testimony and witness: he witnessed to
his dependence on the Father, and he testified that with his coming the kingdom of God had come near. The presence of Jesus to
us gives us an immediate relation to the Father and to the kingdom in him. We cannot first get to know Jesus in himself, and
then go on to know about the Father and about the kingdom from
him afterward. As we have already seen, there is no Jesus to
know apart from his doing the will of the Father, but we must go
on to add that there is also no Jesus to know apart from his proclamation of the kingdom.

Jesus' references to his being sent by the Father and to his doing the will of the Father are scattered throughout the earliest Christian witness. When Jesus is recognized as the Son of the Father, his words and actions in relation to the Father cause no special problems for us. We know something about what a father-son, parent-child relationship is. What Jesus meant when he proclaimed the nearness of the kingdom of God, on the other hand, does cause—and has caused—a number of difficulties. What does "kingdom" mean and in what sense has it drawn near or arrived with Jesus?

Jesus begins his public ministry in Mark by proclaiming, "The time is fulfilled, and the kingdom of God is at hand; repent, and believe in the gospel." (Mk. 1:15) The sense of the statement is that something has already happened with the appearance of Jesus: the time has been fulfilled and the kingdom has drawn near. The same sense of something having already been accomplished is found in Matthew where, after Jesus had healed the blind and speechless demoniac, he states that "if it is by the Spirit of God that I cast out demons, then the kingdom of God has come upon you." (Matt. 12:28) With Jesus the kingdom has already come. Reference to the kingdom of God as already having come near is also found in Luke, with Luke and Matthew sometimes apparently using the same source material. (Cf., Lk. 10:9, 11; 11:20) While a number of other citations could be made from the Gospels, we need not refer to them here. (Cf., Matt. 3:2; 4:17; 10:7; Lk. 21:31)

When most people hear the word "kingdom," a quaint and distant place is apt to be the first association called to their minds. A kingdom should have a king and queen, knights and ladies, walls and towers. Such imagery did make its way into the life of the church at certain periods, but such imagery today, far from being helpful, often lends emphasis to those who think Christianity itself is quaint.

The Greek word translated "kingdom" is most frequently translated these days as the "reign" of God. God's will being done and the presence of his kingdom are the same thing. When, in the Lord's Prayer, we pray for God's kingdom to come and his will to be done on earth as it is in heaven, the same thing is being referred to by the different words "kingdom" and "will."

In order to understand what the kingdom of God (or the kingdom of heaven) is, it will be helpful to say what it is not. The kingdom of God has a location, but it is not a place in the manner it is often thought to be. When we speak of the reign of God, we are speaking of God's will being done in the manner in which people relate to each other in their lives in the world. Because people who relate to each other in God's name are related and located by their bodies, the reign of God is located by those same bodies. That is what we meant when we said the kingdom of God has a location.

Because the kingdom of God is located in the world in the manner we have described, it should not be thought of as a place in itself into which people move by God's favor. The kingdom of heaven is not a celestial country which God will someday float down to earth for his people to enter as their final reward. The kingdom is not a thing in itself, already finished and waiting, that God will give to those who keep themselves unspotted by the world because they withdraw from the world. The kingdom of God exists *in* the actions and relations of human beings as God's people serve and witness in the Spirit of Christ in the world. The Christian God is a relation of Persons to each other, so how could his kingdom be anything but the relation of persons to each other?

It is because the kingdom of God is not a thing in itself waiting to be given to us as a child receives a present that Christ said the kingdom does not come "with observation." (Lk. 17:21) The kingdom does not exist here or there in itself by itself; thus, as Jesus adds, we cannot say, "Lo, here it is," or, "There." The kingdom is not an object in its own right; it is a relationship that exists in something else—it is a certain quality found in the relations of human beings to each other as they live in the Spirit of Christ. The building blocks of the kingdom are the relations of people to each other, not stones mined from heavenly quarries.

Jesus goes on to say that "the kingdom of God is within you." (Lk. 17:21, alternate RSV translation.) The kingdom is within us where the source of our responsible action is rooted; the reign of God exists in us as we will God's will in the Spirit. The kingdom is seen in the way we live time in Christ; it cannot be observed as a self-enclosed place we will one day enter. It is located, and it cannot be itself without location, but it is located by the way we live our bodily lives in the mystical body of Christ.

The fact that the kingdom of God is within us does not mean the kingdom is spiritual and invisible, making no difference in the physical world. The kingdom cannot be in us if it is not discernible in the world by the visible difference we make in the world through our bodies. A human being *is* his or her body. To be a person is to be a body as well as being an extension of time; to be a human person is to be a spatial location as well as an on-going history. We are ourselves only in, through, and as our bodily lives. We are in the world through our bodies as bodies, a fact easily enough proven by our change of status in relation to the world in the event we call death.

Because God's Truth has been embodied in time as we are and is now itself through the living of time, it is impossible to love God as he wants to be loved in a purely contemplative manner. To accept Jesus as the Way is to acknowledge that our most intimate life with God is found in the wholeness of our bodily lives in the world rather than through spiritual intention only. Sitting— even kneeling—is different from walking in the Spirit.

Living the faith of Jesus is our liberation; such living frees us from concern about ourselves, so that we can give our full attention to the reign of God in the world. Accepting our lives in Jesus by living his faith in his Spirit, we are liberated in the present from bondage to the past by the future offered to us in Jesus' resurrection. The joy of being able to live where we are for what we are is the consummate joy of human life; such living will be ours if we are truly followers of Jesus. When we live the reign of God in the world, there is time for things for which there would otherwise be no time in the world; to live in the kingdom of God is to live in the end-time—there is nowhere else to go. We are called to full activity and creativity, but there is nothing to be frantic about because the future is already won in Christ.

When we feel privileged to be with the one we love, we count it a privilege to be with that person simply doing whatever he or she does. The way our love of God shows in the world is to love what God loves in the world. God so loved the world that he sent his Son into the world, and the Son, in turn, told his disciples that he sent them into the world as the Father had sent him. It was in the sending of the disciples to all nations that the risen Jesus told his followers he would be with them to the close of the age. Strange as it might sound at first, we are never more intimately with Jesus than when going to others in his name. Going to others is what Jesus does; we cannot be with him unless we join him in what he is doing. That he lets us join him is his love for us.

8.

Jesus and the Evolution of the Universe

God's creation is forward looking and still going on; evolution has been suggested as a key to understanding God's on-going work in the world—a key that is not tied down to one cultural perspective rather than another. Evolution is seen to involve interrelated dynamic circuits of energy, rather than proceeding by straight-line, linear processes. Evolution, as we participate in it, is a high-energy activity requiring communal support and a source of energy beyond the process itself.

Jesus' constant witness was that the reign of God had appeared with his coming. He heralded the kingdom and introduced it, but God's reign was not consummate with Jesus' ministry on earth or with the resurrection and glorification of Jesus after his crucifixion. That is why, as part of the Easter event, the Spirit was newly poured out upon all flesh to supply the energy necessary for the growth of the kingdom in the world.

More is to come. Living in the Spirit, we help bring about something new in the future, not here yet, beyond us all: the fullness of God's reign on earth. Actualizing the reign of God in the world is a high-energy activity, because forces oppose such actualization; active forces both within and outside of us fight against God's reign, and the inertia of the status quo opposes anything new and creative. Creatively to seek increased justice, respect, and integration in human relationships is opposed by the easier way of not rocking the boat. In our personal lives, as well as in our social lives, we are always tempted to sell the future for the present while forgetting the past. The depletion of our natural resources and the polluting of our environment, expediency instead of statesmanship in politics, profits rather than prudence in industry, illustrate the point we are making. Sex, eating and drinking offer immediate gratification and so can be isolated from larger networks of interrelations; because of the immediate gratification of sensuous delight, its advocacy requires a minimum of witness and personal effort. The inertia of our lives commends it rather than opposing it.

When we discover ourselves in the life of Jesus, we have said, we discover ourselves as participants in something bigger than we are going on in the world. Because of that fact, in the light of our growing knowledge of the universe, we can no longer describe the process into which we are incorporated by our life in the Spirit in terms restricted to one culture alone. God's creative activity transcends cultural relativity in a movement embracing the farthermost reaches of the universe. The singularity of Jesus' historical life must never be compromised, for it is that life which speaks to our lives, but the significance of Jesus' life must not be restricted to one cultural setting or time.

The insight that Jesus' life is significant for all reality is discovered in the New Testament itself, when, in John's Gospel, Jesus is described as the incarnate Word (*logos*), the means by which all things were created and the source of all order in creation. It is now suggested that the evolutionary context, a context extending beyond human culture to the expanding universe, provides the best means of understanding the significance of Jesus today.

Life in the Spirit leads us deeper into the world made by God's love, rather than removing us from it. The kingdom of God is not a city descending from the heavens; it is an interdependent network of relations achieved by God's grace. The reign of God, seen as a network of interrelations, can be understood as the ultimate ecological whole in which everything created is, at one time, accepted for itself and integrated into an all-inclusive dynamic equilibrium with everything else.

Juan Luis Segundo, following suggestions made by Gregory Bateson, is an advocate of understanding Jesus' relevance for us in evolutionary terms. Such terms transcend the culture of Jesus' day, but they do not require that Jesus be removed from his time. Segundo is commonly known as a liberation theologian, but his theological views transcend that school and should not be subsumed under a heading which, to many people, is a political label.[1]

God's creation is not finished and backward-looking; it is forward-looking and still going on. Evolution best describes God's creative process, but evolution is a complex process whose dynamics are found to be very different from the simplistic worldview of past ages. Evolutionary process involves aspects of both change and stability—mutations occur within relatively stable environments—and evolutionary progress is found to be best described in terms of probabilities involving whole populations rather than in terms of specific predictions about specific and isolated individuals.

When all of its complexities are considered, evolution is best understood in terms of circuity, Segundo suggests, rather than in terms of linear, straight-line progression. A circuit "operates through *successive activations and deactivations of energy*," not by one dominating activity alone.[2] In the physical world, there are mechanical circuits and what may be called biological circuits; neither is reducible to the other, but a similarity of function is discovered amidst the differences each system manifests.

A circuit maintains itself in operation through a series of successive events that influence each other. In a circuit, balance must be kept and overload avoided, as different factors come into play at different times. A circuit works through time, making adjustments to different occurrences at different times, rather than proceeding in a straight and uninterrupted line from a point of departure to a goal. Disruptions and unforeseen events play roles in the activity of a circuit; they play no role at all in "linear logic," which goes in a straight, unbroken line from the conception of its premises to the conception of its conclusion.

Until recently, it was thought nature moved in much the same manner in which human beings abstractly inferred conclusions from premises. We are now learning that nature is more complex than that; reality is best described in terms of patterns and fields instead of in terms of simple linear progressions. Considered linearly, it is hard to understand why, once the reign of God was introduced into the world by Jesus, God's rule has not triumphantly won the day, instead of still struggling, as it does, against a hostile and largely unconverted world. Given the appearance of Jesus and the gift of the Spirit, the goal of God's reign and the means of bringing the reign about are present. That being the case, why is the consummate kingdom of God not present in the world? Was Jesus wrong? Was Jesus a fraud? Was the Spirit given? Is the Spirit efficacious?

If, on the other hand, the reign of God, a network of relations, is understood dynamically in terms of circuitry rather than in terms of straight-line deductions, such questions as we have just asked lose much of their force. It is a matter of understanding how God works. Disappointment may arise from our lack of understanding rather than from God's impotence. If all reality comes from one Source, all reality hangs together, and, as in so many instances, we must not substitute our expectations for God's mind.

Because of the complexity of the evolutionary process, long periods of time are necessary to discern direction and significance. Multitudes of energy patterns related in innumerably different circumstances are involved in the evolutionary circuit. Events beyond our control and circumstances we cannot foresee constantly occur in the world; even with the grace of God we cannot move in a straight-line manner from the proclamation of the kingdom by Jesus to it's full realization. The consummation of God's reign involves interrelations of the whole of creation, not just the intentions of isolated individuals.

A nonlinear progression of the kingdom will not be a discouragement if we understand how circuits work. An initial change, first noted in but one place among the interrelations of the universe, ultimately affects everything in the interconnected web of reality constituting the universe. Once a new threshold of interrelations is introduced in the world, as Jesus introduced the kingdom, its progression will not be easy or direct in the face of the multitude of uncontrolled factors it encounters. In our social environment, for example, because the kingdom is a new pattern of relationships, it will have to struggle against the entrenched opposition of old habits and expectations. It will have to struggle against those who are getting what they want in the old way. Not everyone wants change. Free wills oppose God's will. Should the God who is love destroy the freedom of those who oppose him?

In the world of human relations, the comfort and security of the familiar, cheap mass energy that produces the ease of the status quo will drag against the creative action of God's reign. The kingdom of God is the reign of God's love in the world, a love that is creative and challenging. Such love fights against the drag of the status quo of the universe as a closed system. Christian love is the high-energy needed to actualize God's rule in the world. The energy necessary cannot come from us; we can only receive it as a gift from beyond us. Fortunately, it is not our responsibility or our resources that Christian love taps; God's love is the source of the power we need—God moves first. God comes to us, loving us, and because his love for us is *his*, it is so much more than we are that it overflows us into our relations with others. That is how the kingdom grows. Our only responsibility is to accept the love God offers us in Jesus. For a Christian, confronted with the unknown factors of life in the world and confronted with circumstances over which he or she has no control, Jesus is all there is. But when Jesus is all there is, Jesus is all; his presence enables us to continue our witness in his name, no matter what unexpectedly happens to our plans. Especially in an evolving universe, the singularity of Jesus' life is all important.

The kingdom of God, since it is an open and caring interrelation of persons—and so a community of persons—may also be considered, with appropriate modifications, a circuit of circuits. There is a sense in which a person is a dynamic circuit of energy, an analogy which, if allowed, makes a community of persons a circuit of circuits. In such terms, a society that devalues persons, treating them as objects, using them mechanically and impersonally, is a low-energy society dominated by the drag of its own weight. Its future is the death of sameness. Jesus is the love of God, God's creative energy encountering and overcoming the repetition of the present, showing that the universe is not a closed system whose end has no significance.

With the advent of personal life in the evolution of the universe, a threshold of being was passed which exceeded in a unique and singular manner the being of the physical universe as a whole. Persons can question the nature of physical reality and ask the question why there is any physical reality at all. In questioning the reason for the existence of the universe, persons transcend the universe—which is the reason why God is able to call us as persons to participate in his creative action in the universe. Participation in God's act of creation is the actualizing of the reign of God in the world through life in the Spirit.

The actualization of the kingdom takes time and energy, for such creative activity must constantly fight against the low-energy appeal of sensual satisfaction already available in the present. Working in the grace of the risen Christ towards better interrelations of persons in God's justice and peace does not have the immediate appeal of a couple of cocktails followed by a big dinner. The pay-off does not come so quickly. Living from the future towards the future, as Christians live in faith and hope, opposes what is now known as the "natural" inclinations of both human beings and the physical universe. High resolve is necessary to sustain witness to God's reign in the face of constant opposition. The material world offers no inducement to such a life; in fact, such a life may be the very thing making material comfort impossible. Witness to Jesus makes martyrs in the world; it does not produce examples of easy living by conspicuous consumption.

Actions promoting the kingdom of God are *personal* actions— actions only persons can undertake. They are actions which intensify personhood, emphasizing the dimensions of personal being that transcend our physical dimensions. Faith, hope, love, commitment, thanksgiving, concern, sacrifice, and joy cannot be described in physical or mathematical terms, even though each activity mentioned has physical correlates in our bodily lives. God's kingdom can grow in the world only as persons reinforce persons in the intensity of their relation with the person, Jesus. Christian witness is a shared witness; from the sharing comes an important part of its strength. Christian witness begins with Jesus sharing himself with us in the gift of the Spirit. As isolated individuals, we can get drowsy and fall asleep after a big meal, but we can be agents of the reign of God only as we live together, dying to individualism, opening ourselves to the presence of God and of each other in the Spirit. Sleep is isolation, as is death; life is communion and presence.

The high-energy work of the kingdom requires mutual support and nurture as its source; constantly sharing their witness with each other in the Spirit is the means by which agents of the kingdom rise above the introverted isolation of sensual ease. The Word of God calls people out of themselves into community with him and with each other in him. Such living is our salvation, for it is the way we are saved from ourselves and what we are by ourselves. Only as members of the community God calls into existence by his Word can people be agents of God's reign in the world. The energy needed for the task is high, but that energy's availability is immediate and present in the gift of the Spirit of the resurrected Christ.

Notes

1. Segundo has written a five-volume series under the general title, *Jesus of Nazareth Yesterday and Today*. The whole series is most suggestive for our discussion, especially volumes I, III, and V. I have principally drawn from volume V, *An Evolutionary Approach to Jesus of Nazareth*, translated by John Drury (Maryknoll: Orbis Books, 1988), in this chapter.

2. Segundo, *An Evolutionary Approach to Jesus of Nazareth*, p. 71.

9.

Flesh, Blood, and Creation

It is significant that the life of Jesus is available to us as we eat his flesh and drink his blood. "Flesh" and "blood" had special meanings in Jesus' day. The church, the community of faith, is a eucharistic community; its structure is one with the basic structure of the universe and makes a creative difference in the universe.

Jesus, the Word of God, calls us out of ourselves into community with him and with each other. It is only in community, not as isolated individuals, we have said, that the high-energy work of the kingdom can be accomplished. In the Spirit who made Jesus the Christ, the anointed one, the Messiah, God calls his people into a high-energy community to continue the activity of Jesus' life in the world today. The visible church is the community of people who recognize the on-going life of Jesus in the world and who consciously identify themselves with that life.

The church is the community of faith in which people knowingly give themselves to the intimate, personal life of Jesus. They support and encourage each other in that life, but more basic than that is the nurture and strength they receive for their life in Christ by the new food of the kingdom, the bread which comes down from heaven, the bread of life. (Jn. 6:41)

The community called together by God's Word to do God's will is strengthened for its work by special food. It is in the life of Jesus that God's will is newly lived in the world and, Christians believe, it is only by participating in the very life Jesus lived that God's will can continue to be done in the world.

That Jesus' life is available to us and can become the source of the life we live is the principal significance of the sixth chapter of John's Gospel. Jesus there calls himself the bread of life, "the living bread which came down from heaven; if anyone eats of this bread, he will live for ever; and the bread which I shall give for the life of the world is my flesh." (Jn. 6:48, 51) Jesus goes on to say, "Truly, truly, I say to you, unless you eat the flesh of the Son of man and drink his blood, you have no life in you. . . . For my flesh is food indeed, and my blood is drink indeed. He who eats my flesh and drinks my blood abides in me, and I in him." (Jn. 6:53-56)

Even though the words of Jesus we have just quoted were not spoken at the Last Supper, Christians throughout the ages have understood them to convey the meaning of that Supper, the holy eucharist. The eucharist is not just a service in a church building. It is rightly said to be the central act of Christian worship, but it is more than that: it is the source and summary of all Christian living in the world.

The Christian life begins in something that happened in the world, the life of Jesus, and the eucharist—itself a gift—exists to enable that founding event to continue to be present and to make a difference in the world. Through the centuries, Christians have come to God's table, called by God's Word, to offer thanksgiving for God's redeeming love, and to eat the sacramental food of the new creation so that they could go into the world as renewed agents of God's kingdom.

The church truly is a eucharistic community. The holy eucharist is an action, a way of living, not a service that is sometimes put on and other times totally put off. The eucharist is rather the intensification and source of a life continuously lived—the life of Jesus, as his life is still lived in the world, not beyond it. In the eucharist, the action of Jesus' life is located in a specific place, just as his life was located by his physical body while he physically lived on earth.

It is of utmost importance to recognize the significance of Jesus' saying that it is his flesh we should eat and his blood we should drink. In the prologue to John's Gospel, it is said that "the Word became flesh." (1:14) Early Christians were accused of cannibalism by the use of the word "flesh," and even today many people are made uneasy by the term. We must understand what "flesh" meant to the Hebrew mind. "Flesh," as it was used in biblical times, was a much more inclusive word than "body." Rather than being but one aspect of the body, as "flesh" would be understood by the Greeks, for the Hebrew mind "flesh" meant the whole human person living under the conditions of the world and subject to the accidents, temptations, limitations, weaknesses, sickness, and death everyone experiences in the world. The Word did not just take on a body, the Word of God spoken in Jesus is spoken in a life identical with our lives in the world. God in Jesus was with his first disciples and is now with us under precisely the conditions of the life they lived and we live.

God in Jesus comes to us within our time; he does not stay beyond it. God is with us not only where we live but as we live. When Jesus tells us to eat his flesh, he is telling us that he makes his life in the world available for us to eat so that his life can enter our life as its food! We can eat his life as his gift to us because he has made himself available to us by first tasting death for us. The Epistle to the Hebrews says that in the grace of God Jesus came so that "he might taste death for every one." (Heb. 2:9) He has eaten the bitterest fruit of our life so that we can eat the victory of his life.

We should also understand the significance of Jesus' saying we should drink his blood. We miss the shock that the Jews and early disciples of Jesus' day experienced when the eucharistic chalice was said to hold the blood of Christ. In the dietary and ritualistic laws of Judaism, nothing was more fiercely forbidden than the drinking of blood. The life of an animal was identified with its blood, and that life belongs to God alone. When an animal was sacrificed, an animal later to be eaten by worshippers, the blood was always drained out of the carcass and poured on the ground in homage to God; only after what was God's was given to God could the flesh be prepared for human beings and eaten by them. The drinking of blood could not even be symbolized in the rituals of Judaism. Such a thing was blasphemous.

The New Covenant announced by the Word of God in Jesus completely overturned the Law of the Old Covenant. A revolutionary change occurred. In no way could the revolution be more dramatically indicated than in identifying the consecrated wine of the holy Eucharist—the blood of the grape—with the blood of Jesus. The principal taboo of Judaism became the means of grace—it became God's will—in Christianity. In Christianity blood is the life too, but now it is the new life God offers his people in Christ.

In the holy eucharist, otherwise known as the holy mysteries, the sacramental body and blood of Christ convey the life of Christ to those who eat and drink them. The life of Christ is the Spirit of Christ—the Spirit of God. The Spirit is associated with the blood of Christ, and Paul even speaks of the Spirit being drunk by those who have been baptized into the one body. (I Cor. 12:13)

At the institution of the holy eucharist, as recorded in the Gospel of Mark, Jesus, we are told, "took bread, and blessed, and broke it, and gave it to them, and said, 'Take; this is my body.' And he took a cup, and when he had given thanks he gave it to them, and they all drank of it. And he said to them, 'This is my blood of the covenant, which is poured out for many. Truly, I say to you, I shall not drink again of the fruit of the vine until that day when I drink it new in the kingdom of God.'" (14:22-25) By making reference to a new drinking of wine in the kingdom of God to which he was going, the meal at which Christ was presiding became associated with a meal and a company beyond it. In the eucharist we eat the first fruits of the age to come; we participate in the glory of God's will fully being done on earth as it is in heaven.

Because heaven is essentially a community of people participating in the communion of Persons who are God, a banquet, the
celebration of community, has frequently been used as a symbol
for heaven. The eucharistic banquet may thus be seen as a participation in the future messianic banquet which takes place in
heaven. It was with such an understanding that early Christians
heard Jesus say that "men will come from east and west, from
north and south, and sit at table in the kingdom of God." (Lk.
13:29)

The community of people who respond to the Word of God in
Jesus comprise the church. The church is commonly known as
the mystical body of Christ in the world and, as we have been
indicating, the church is most intensely itself in the holy mysteries, otherwise known as the holy eucharist. God's people are
most themselves in the holy mysteries when the one Christ, in his
one presence, gives himself to his people, nourishing them as living members of his one body, and loving them, as the Father
loves him, in the gift of the Spirit. God's giving of his own interior life of love to us through the Son in the Spirit creates a
community of self-giving—a community that finds both its identity and its strength in the holy eucharist.

Paul told the Corinthians that the new creation they received
in Christ was their reconciliation with God who, in Christ, gave
them the ministry of reconciliation in the world. "Therefore, if
anyone is in Christ, he is a new creation; the old has passed
away, behold the new has come. All this is from God, who
through Christ reconciled us to himself and gave us the ministry
of reconciliation; that is, in Christ God was reconciling the world
to himself, not counting their trespasses against them, and en-
trusting to us the message of reconciliation. So we are ambassa-
dors for Christ, God making his appeal through us." (II Cor.
5:17-20)

"God making his appeal through us" is a striking claim; it is a
basic truth of Christian faith—as true today as it was true in
Paul's day—but we too often miss the full implications of Paul's
words. As believers participate in the new life of Christ in the

Spirit, not only do they become a new creation, they become agents of God's on-going and evolving creation of the universe. The appeal God makes through us is not a simple social request and our ambassadorship is not a mere political appointment; the reconciliation we receive and which we are to impart through our redeemed lives in the world involves nothing less than the basic fabric of the universe itself. We take part in the evolving structure of all reality.

The community of faith we have been describing, visibly known as the church, is not an assembly of human beings who, in their bodies, are externally related to one another. Christian community is a personal activity, a corporate act of thanksgiving offered to God by the community of faith for the new life God makes available to human beings in Jesus. The community of God's people is an interrelation of the activities of every believer's life with the activities of every other believer's life, integrated in the activity of the Spirit of Jesus' life. Christian community is a personal activity of interrelated personal activities. So understood, Christian living takes on its full significance in our best understanding of the universe today.

Christian community is not an assembly of bodies externally related to one another, and, in fact, neither our world nor the universe as a whole can be properly understood as an assembly of bodies externally related to each other. As physics now conceives the universe, the universe and our world within it are not made up of solid objects; instead, physical reality is better thought of as a web of interconnected energy patterns.

The elements of physical reality are no longer conceived as submicroscopic objects or things that, assembled together, make up the bigger objects we perceive through our senses. Instead of the universe being thought of as a collection of objects, it is better thought of as a network of relations. There is no such thing as an isolated individual, as physics now conceives the universe. The universe is found to be a huge network of interrelations, and everything in the universe can be known only in its relationship with everything else. What we perceive as objects are structured bundles of energy, and all the bundles are held together in an interconnected web that imparts a unity and structure to the whole which is more than the sum of its physical parts. Nothing can be known apart from its interrelationship with everything else. There is a communal aspect to all reality.

We understand the world differently today than it was understood in biblical times. In earlier days reality was thought to be more static and fixed than we know it today. The stars, for example, were thought to be permanent, even regarded as gods, who guided navigators and otherwise influenced life in the world. Although physical objects were taken to be static substances, it was also thought that all of the universe, even in its fixed and most stable forms, would be brought to a cataclysmic end by a mighty act of God. In the end, in the "last days," God would show his supremacy even over the supremacy of the fixed stars.

In biblical times a "big bang" was anticipated at the end of the world. Our understanding of the universe, even though it is now questioned in some quarters, is that the big bang occurred at the beginning of the universe. Whether the physical universe began in a big bang or not, we know the universe is constantly expanding as if it resulted from a cosmic explosion, and we know that constant change and activity are occurring everywhere. Instead of thinking of the stars as stable substances or immortal gods, we know them to be bubbling cauldrons of energy. We no longer think of things as static substances; we know them to be patterns of pulsating energy. Everything is in flux—even the church and society. More change surrounds us than many people can stand. We want to call a halt to the change so that we can find a place to stand, but where can it be found? Empires, political systems, civilizations rise and fall. The statement of a storied potentate, a statement he made on every occasion and supplied to him by his wise men so that he would be known as the wisest king who ever reigned, applies with additional force today: "This, too, will pass."

Christians believe that God, in Jesus of Nazareth, comes into our changing world to show us that not everything caught up in the endless round of beginnings and endings of the world will be lost. In Jesus, God enters time to show us a way to live our changing lives that is more than the endless change of the world. What is it? A life of love—of concern for others; such a life has a meaning and glory from beyond the world, a meaning and glory that arise out of the life of God himself.

In Jesus we see that human nature has a meaning and a purpose beyond itself. Self-fulfillment is not our goal. It is our defeat. Mark Twain once said the worst advice anyone could receive was "to be yourself." We are called to be more than our-selves, for our life in the world has a meaning beyond the world.

The Word of God spoken in Jesus does not only tell us that our lives in the world have a meaning beyond the world; just as importantly, the life of Jesus tells us the correlative truth that our lives have no meaning beyond the world apart from our lives in the world. The Word became flesh to show us that our perfection does not consist in withdrawing from the world, but rather in participating in the world's on-going creation—the spread of the kingdom.

When Peter, James, and John went with Jesus up the Mount of the Transfiguration, and they saw him mystically transfigured be-fore them, the meaning of the event was that, even while Jesus was in the world, he was more than the world. When the disci-ples saw Jesus talking to Elijah, who stands for the prophetic tradition—all the prophets—of Israel, and to Moses, the great de-liverer of God's people from their slavery in Egypt, the early church understood that, in Jesus, the prophetic and redemptive vocation of Israel, known in the prophets and Moses, was not only fulfilled but infinitely exceeded.

The faithful see Jesus as the one who does more than save people from slavery in the world; he saves people from the ulti-mate slavery of the world, from the bondage of death. Living our lives in the Spirit of Jesus' life is our transfiguration. That is how our lives change. When people see the Spirit of God in us through our concern for others, they see, as Peter, James, and

John saw of Jesus on the Mount, that we are more than ourselves even while we are in the world.

Flannery O'Connor was once asked what made a good short story. She replied that it took two ingredients, meaning and muscle—and she added that the meaning must be in the muscle. Our lives are stories, and the same thing is true of them: their meaning must be in their muscle. Meaning must be in life, not behind, above, or below it. Miss O'Connor's remark contains a valuable theological insight also; it can help us understand the Incarnation. When God's Word became flesh, God's meaning was put in the muscle! God's Word put the meaning of the world in the world; those of us living in the world—and whom does that leave out?—cannot find God's meaning apart from the world.

The freedom God offers us in our redemption in Christ makes no difference apart from the world, for the world is the sum of things that make a difference to us. The world is the "reality test" of the release and freedom we find in Jesus. Because God's Word to us can only be found in the fleshly Jesus, the freedom God offers us in him must be as real as the world—and that freedom can be shown only in the world. The freedom we are offered in Christ is freedom to grasp reality, acknowledge it, face it, engage it, accept it, change it—not escape it. We can do all that because, in Christ, we do not fear reality. The fear of reality, not reality itself, is what Jesus removes from us.

The Christian witness is that although God's freedom is as real as the world and must be lived in the world, the freedom is too new to be contained in the world. The freedom we have in Christ is so new that it needs—and thus makes—a new world. That is why Paul tells the Galatians that it is "for freedom [that] Christ has set us free." (5:1) Freedom is not *for* anything. Anything it would be *for* would stand outside it and be untouched by it. God's freedom is as real as the world, but it makes a world of its own; that is why we cannot help participating in God's creation, as agents of the kingdom, in the Spirit of Jesus. To accept the freedom given by the Spirit of Christ is to be reborn; everything in life is changed, because everything is done in a new way and is seen in a new light.

God's meaning and God's freedom are themselves only when we live them as Jesus lived them. With Jesus we celebrate a life, not an idea; and that celebration is meant to fill a life, not occasionally interrupt it as a release from boredom. To participate in God's on-going creation is not a sometimes activity. It is a constant celebration.

10.

The Spiritual Life

The spiritual life is a life recognizing the inter-connectedness of all reality in the presence of God. It is life in the Spirit. There is a difference between information processing and personal communication; in the latter, we become more than ourselves in the presence of another person. We can do more—and are more—in the presence of another person than we can do—or be—alone. In the Spirit, "following Jesus" is an intimate presence rather than an external tagging along after someone beyond us.

It is one thing to say energy is available to us in the gift of the Spirit of the resurrected Christ and another thing to have the statement make sense in a manner helpful to us in the living of our lives. Although remarks may be well-intentioned, pious talk is different from actual help. How, we may wonder, is the energy of the Spirit really available to us and, if it is, how do we get it?

The presence of the Spirit in our lives depends upon our being able to have a spiritual life. What does such a life mean?

In its full meaning for Christians, the spiritual life is life in the Spirit. That is not to say, however, that a spiritual dimension of our lives is found only in our relation to God. When human persons are truly present to each other as persons, the presence is possible only because of a spiritual dimension of human beings, although physical location and physical means are also involved.

God's presence to us is different from—but similar to—our presence to each other as persons, and his presence is the presence we are meant to mirror in our relations with each other.

It is often said that human beings have a body, mind, and spirit. The distinctions are not as helpful as many suppose, however, because they make the spiritual life sound mindless and as if it had nothing to do with the body. Of course both alternatives are false. The spiritual life involves our highest rational abilities and our embodied life in the world or it does not involve *us*; we are not ourselves without our minds and bodies. Our spiritual lives involve a conscious relationship with something we recognize to be true, and our rational nature alone in its mental activities can recognize the truth as truth; in addition, as Christians, the love we return to the Word of Love incarnate is impossible without our bodies.

There is great stress these days on the wholeness of the human person, and the emphasis is well made. A human being is a whole, but a whole consisting of different aspects that can be variously highlighted when looked at from different points of view. A human person has, for example, physical and mental, material and nonmaterial, emotional and rational dimensions.

The most basic distinction found within human nature is that between the material and nonmaterial aspects of our being; since anything nonmaterial is spiritual, "physical" and "spiritual" are terms we may use to designate the fundamental composition we recognize in ourselves. Our bodies and physical aspects obviously belong to the material dimension we have noted; our nonmaterial dimension may be variously referred to as either our soul or spirit. The soul (or spirit) of a person is a nonmaterial structure that gives unity to the different aspects of human nature we discern within a person. Within the wholeness of human life we can distinguish physical and chemical components; an organic dimension that includes nutrition, growth, and reproduction; animal characteristics such as sensation, feeling, and locomotion; and the highest personal abilities of reasoning and willing. The soul is a unifying structure actualizing those dimensions of our being in such a manner that a single person exists. The soul is a principle of unity.

As "spirit" is used in the spiritual life, it is not a faculty separate and distinct from mind or reason; instead, it is the mindful, rational dimension of our being that can recognize the interconnectedness of all human beings and of all reality in the presence of God. Our spirit or soul is that dimension of our being that is open to the otherness of God and of the rest of creation, an openness that rejoices in and unites with the otherness of God and other people—instead of withdrawing from that otherness, defending itself against it, and trying to subdue it. Through our spirit and in our spiritual lives we express love, seeking communion and union with others in their difference. In our spiritual lives we want to be with others without damaging them, respecting them for who they are; our spiritual presence to another in love actually encourages the other person's otherness to become more itself. In our spiritual dimension, we can live in a community of presence that is supportive, nurturing, refreshing, tension-releasing, nonthreatening, quieting, respecting, dignifying, consoling, fitting—rather than seeking self-fulfillment in a "space which is mine"—a space different from yours externally relating us to each other and negatively defining us as we exclude each other.

At the spiritual level we can be intentionally with anyone anywhere through the exercise of our will and attention. Physical distance does not make personal presence impossible, as lovers testify. Lovers prefer the physical presence of each other, but physical separation does not keep them from each other's presence in the center of their being. Distance can even bring lovers closer together, and many a lover has never felt closer to his beloved than when they were apart. To establish true spiritual contact with another any place is to enter a network of reality that can be extended everywhere. It was in such a manner that the disciples were moved by the presence of Jesus in their lives.

Being spiritually present with God and other persons is not an easy task in our competitive, externally related society; spiritual presence is an intimate presence, and many people do not know how to be intimate today. "Intimate relations" are nowadays taken as a synonym for sexual relations, which need not be intimate at all. A teeming industry that has produced workshops, seminars, audio tapes, books, and private counselling sessions has grown up to help people expand their personal horizons and learn how to relate to others in a truly personal manner. The religious end of the market is directed towards helping people relate to God in an interior, personal way. Books on the spiritual life and methods of meditation are many but, similar to psychological counselling, there is a common core of practice that belies the multitude of formally labeled systems.

Almost all spiritual methods agree that, as the first step to being present with God or anyone else, we must collect ourselves in order to be our complete selves in the meeting. This step is often described as "centering ourselves" in ourselves, that is, recalling ourselves to ourselves and not letting ourselves be spread out in the world. To be spiritually present with a person we must be present with our whole selves, nothing missing, no attention or desire lacking. The person we want to be with is our sole desire. It is the type of presence we desire in love.

We can have such a presence with Jesus. Because he lives, his presence is available to us, but we must open ourselves to him and gather ourselves together so that all of us can be with him. Our activities so spread us out in the world that such centering of ourselves is often difficult for us, but it is not a difficulty we have only with God. How often are we truly and completely in the presence of another person in the world? We have trouble truly being persons with each other; thus we know other people only in a functional and impersonal way. We relate to others only because of what they can do for us, and many people know themselves only by the functions they perform. People so identify themselves with what they do that when they no longer have a job to go to they are totally lost; their identity as persons is found only in their work. When they can no longer find their identity in their business or profession, they are nothing, and they prove it by dying shortly after retirement.

Our personal presence with Jesus is not unlike the spiritual presence we may have with each other. When we are truly present with another person, each of us freely gives himself or herself to the other by the attention bestowed on the other. Reciprocal personal presence is always a gift, and, in the Christian experience, God as a gift is God the Spirit. The Father gives himself to the Son as Spirit, and the Son, sent by the Father, is given to us in the Spirit. The difficult thing about the Christian life is accepting the presence of Jesus in our lives with unlimited receptivity, that is, as nothing but a gift. We cannot accept the gift of Jesus' presence in the power of the Spirit for our purposes; Jesus is with us for who he is, not for what we want. Jesus comes to serve but not to be used; he comes to serve the Father and to show us how to serve the Father, not to be used by us. His presence brings something new to us—himself.

Our presence with Jesus is the presence of God's life in our lives. God's life will show in the way we live and in what we do; it will show in the way we achieve our purposes, but it cannot be obtained as the means of achieving our purposes. It can only be accepted as the gift of God's presence to us. An act of our will is necessary for us to be present with God—we have to let ourselves be with him—but that is not the same thing as trying to project God's presence into our lives by our will alone. God is always present with us in Jesus for who he—God—is, doing what he does. We must will to live with him at that level if we want to be with him.

Our spiritual presence with Jesus is the immediate presence of his inner self in our lives. His presence is the Spirit of the Father moving us, for, as the Christ, Jesus is the one whose life is nothing but the movement of the Spirit in the world. To live with Jesus is to be moved as he was moved: we live in the Spirit of the Father. We spiritually share his energy.

There is a difference between communication that is no more than externally transmitted information processing and communion that is the spiritual presence of persons to each other through their mutual indwelling. The former is often mistaken for personal communion, but there is a great difference between the two. Communication that is no more than information processing is a source of reaction among the individuals taking part in it: upon receipt of new information, individuals involved in the process react on the basis of the internal energy already found within them. Their action and reaction are limited by their present resources. People or nations who relate to each other only by what each has externally observed—or heard—about the other are a case in point.

Communication that is the communion of persons who spiritually indwell each other is a new spring of action and energy arising from their shared presence. Our own experience testifies to the fact that we become more and are able to do more in the presence of another person than we are or can do by ourselves alone. Learning to walk is the overcoming of our fear of falling by the presence of mother and her out-stretched arms. I remember a philosophy professor of mine one day saying, immediately after he had responded to a student's question, "I didn't know I knew that!" The presence of the class had brought him beyond himself.

We become more ourselves—and more than ourselves—with the encouraging help and presence of another person. Such presence is the content of the Christian life of those who live with Jesus as the pioneer and author of their faith. Such spiritual identity with the risen Jesus was the source of the new strength Paul found in his life after his conversion; it enabled him to write to the Philippians: "Not that I complain of want; for I have learned, in whatever state I am, to be content. I know how to abound; in any and all circumstances I have learned the secret of facing plenty and hunger, abundance and want. I can do all things in him who strengthens me." (Phil 4:11-13) Because of his presence with Jesus, Paul found the strength of the risen Jesus in his life.

Others have also found Jesus' strength in their lives, but to find it, they, as Paul, had to acknowledge their complete dependence on it. Christian "finding" is "receiving." We want the findings in our lives to be our inventions, something we are responsible for, something we have done for ourselves, our achievement. Self-sufficiency, not total dependence, is the goal

of worldly living, but such living is precisely what Jesus overcame when he said he had overcome the world. (Jn. 16:33) How
did Jesus overcome the world? By his absolute dependence on
the Father. As we will say over and over again, it is ourselves we
need to be saved from: we need only remember the car coming
towards us in our lane.

We find Jesus by accepting him as he comes to us, sent by the
Father. The truth of the matter, I am afraid, is that we are not
very accepting people. We often need to be shaken in our lives in
order to come to ourselves and to see our lives in their true perspective. A cancer diagnosis can offer such a jolt.

> I awakened from anesthesia to be told that the biopsy
> was malignant; I must have a modified radical mastec-
> tomy to save my life. There seemed to be no way
> around this awful truth, only the necessity of summon-
> ing the courage to deal with it. This was not my first
> encounter with grief or loss, but it was the first time I
> had to face the absolute reality of my own mortality.
> This crisis could not be avoided; the cancer cells were
> inside me, and I must lose a part of myself. What if I
> lost all of me and died in surgery or soon after—would
> I still exist, somehow, as me? Suddenly I found my very
> existence threatened, body and soul. The effort of trying
> to make some sense out of what was happening to me
> challenged my faith and trust, leaving me angry and
> afraid, in a veritable spiritual identity crisis.

> The psalm on that Palm Sunday began, "My God, my
> God, why have you forsaken me? and are so far from
> my cry and from the words of my distress? O my God, I
> cry in the daytime, but you do not answer; by night as
> well, but I find no rest. . . . Be not far from me, for
> trouble is near, and there is none to help." The tears
> streamed down my face, uncontrollably, as I tried to
> read the psalm with the rest of the parishioners. In my
> anguish and through my tears I saw my eight-year-old
> daughter's face, lovely and innocent, as she sat in the

choir. My six-year-old son, sitting close beside me, had fear and confusion in his eyes as he saw my tears. My heart was breaking. What would happen to my children if I died while they were so young? This question caused me the most pain. Although I felt very close and connected to many friends and family, paradoxically I felt all alone.

Shortly afterwards, she continues:

In contrast to the desperate distress and anguish of Psalm 22, I remembered the words of comfort found in Psalm 23: "The Lord is my shepherd; I shall not be in want. . . . He revives my soul. . . . Though I walk through the valley of the shadow of death, I shall fear no evil; for you are with me. . . ."

The presence of another person enables us to be more than we are by ourselves. Jesus' agony in time, as he recited the words of the 22nd Psalm from the cross, was one with the agony in time of the young mother; because of that, he was available to her within her need—he did not offer her merely verbal comfort from a state of unperturbed heavenly bliss. Jesus walked with her, step by step, in the journey she was being forced to make.

Jesus was with my friend as her companion, but he was more than that—he was also ahead of her as her guide. He had gone the way before, so his presence with her was also the presence of his victory over the death she feared. Because of God's love having entered time in Jesus, the reality of the fear we know in time is the key to the reality of Jesus' victory over what we fear. Christianity does not battle reality with wishes; it battles reality with reality.

Another friend of mine, this time a man, was told there was a good chance he had a cancer and that a biopsy would be necessary. Introspective by nature with a tendency towards anxiety, he was astonished at how peaceful he was during the period of uncertainty while the test was being run. It was totally unlike him, he reports. He later said that for the first time he realized what an intimately liberating thing it was truly to follow Jesus. Following, he discovered, is not an external relationship; it is an internal presence.

To follow is to go where someone else has gone before, but to have the person who has gone before be present with you, as you go, is the gift of success at the beginning of a venture. My friend said that by giving all of himself up, he truly let Jesus lead him; there was nothing he could worry about because all of him was being led. Jesus was with my friend in my friend's present, but, because it was the resurrected Jesus who was with him, the future already won by Jesus was also in my friend's present. The future Jesus has already won redeemed the present of my friend.

The presence of the risen Jesus in our lives makes—or offers—a difference to every person in the world in a singular, intimate way. The infinite God loves each person for the unique person he or she is, but God's love in Christ is not restricted to individuals as individuals.

Jesus' life is the compassion of God come into the world to reconcile people to God and to each other in God. The kingdom of God introduced by Jesus is the compassionate interrelation of God with his people and of his people with each other in the power of his Spirit. The whole creation is an interconnected network of relations; our "spiritual life" is where the interconnectedness should be most evident. It is in our spiritual lives that the interdependent structure of reality should never be lost to isolation and separation, for the presence of God in our lives is our source of overcoming isolation and separation. It is in our spiritual ability to be present to others in their otherness that God calls us to be agents of his reign in his continuing creation, for God's love so revels in the richness of others that he creates others to revel in. That is why only love can create; love that is almighty calls others into existence just so they can share in the love that created them. Love is a free giving that presupposes nothing; thus it is the only act that can account for the absolute beginning of the universe.

Christian love is a spiritual act recognizing the coherence of creation in God's love and willing to extend that unity through the compassion of our lives in the Spirit. The interrelation of everything in the universe with everything else is a fact of reality known even to physical science; the interrelation is everywhere, but the personal awareness of it is not. Living the awareness of reality's basic structure in a life open to God in the faith of Jesus is our spiritual fulfillment. It is the case for Christianity.

11.

Certainty about Jesus

Our knowledge of the historical Jesus is certain enough to enable us to live time in our times as he lived time in his times. The Christian life is a life of witness. That witness must be made everywhere and at all times by Christians, for through the witness new initial conditions are introduced into the dynamic equilibrium of the world that are the means by which the kingdom grows. There is a Christian, as well as a meteorological, "butterfly effect."

We have been making our case for Christianity as honestly as we can: we have stressed Christianity's historical origin and nature, and we have tried to show the reasonableness of being a Christian in the world in which we live.

Because everything Christian depends on Jesus, nothing is more important than the fact that Jesus lived in the world under the same conditions we do, thus making his life one with ours. Let us look more closely at what we know about the historical Jesus and how we know it.

It has been a given in Christianity from its earliest time that knowledge of Jesus is possible only through the witness others have made to him. That is true of any historical personage to a large extent, but totally true of anyone who did not write documents that have been preserved. The exceptional thing about witness to Jesus has been the difference he made in the lives of those who testify to him. There is no doubt that some witness to Jesus is exaggerated. Exaggeration in any testimony must be rooted out; but in some instances the rooting out may reveal why the exaggeration occurred. In its total context, the reason for an exaggeration may itself give a valid insight into the person or event that was the subject of the exaggeration. In any case, if Jesus was the Christ, he came into the world in order to influence others; knowledge about him will come from that influence. The biggest problem would be if Jesus were the Christ, and he influenced no one so that we could not know about him through others.

The more we know about Jesus in his time and place, the more located he is, the more he helps us in our time and place—even though our world is different from his. To be a person is to be located; human life is always a perspective. We are helped by someone who lives under the same conditions we do, not by someone who does not know our problems. The more we know about the concrete conditions of Jesus' life, the more he can help us live our lives. He does not come to live a life different from ours which, because of its difference, can be of no help to us. As the pioneer of our faith, he must live in his time under the same conditions we live in our time. The question for many is, "Can we know the actual, historical Jesus with enough certainty and detail for him to enter our lives as a real person and change them? Do we know enough about Jesus to be able to live with him as a person?"

What can we say with surety about Jesus from the varied witness we have to him? A summary of present scholarly research offers us the following. There is no doubt that Jesus lived on this earth, that he experienced a special relationship with God as his Father, and that he proclaimed the presence of the reign of God. There is also no reason to doubt that he was crucified by the Romans on the charge of being a political rebel or insurrectionist, and there is no doubt that, in the earliest witness to him, it was claimed that he was raised from the dead and, now living with the Father, gives the Spirit of God to those who receive him in faith.

We also know with certainty that Jesus taught by parables, short stories comparing structural relationships between persons (or between persons and things) that invite interpretation and application in the lives of those who hear the stories. When a person enters into the structural comparison suggested by a parable, a situation is created that can be located anywhere. Thus parabolic meaning never grows old and its possible content is never exhausted. Its significance is never limited to one time and place.

The holiness of God was the primary concern of the Judaism of Jesus' day; that concern about God led to overwhelming concern about purity in the people who worshipped him. The Essenes, whom we know primarily through the Dead Sea Scrolls, were a renewal movement that sought purity by withdrawing from society into isolated communities in the wilderness. The Pharisees, about whom we read so much in the Gospels, had a similar desire for purity but, instead of withdrawing from society, they wanted to transform society through the stringent enforcement of tithes and purity laws. In contrast to achieving God's will either through exclusivist communities or legalistic requirements, Jesus came to call people into a community of acceptance and compassion. In his parables and in his life, Jesus condemned treating people as objects either in the name of the Law (which would amount to idolatry of the Law) or because of unconcern (which would be an idolatry of the self). Having come to do the will of the Father, Jesus, by his life, showed the Father to be compassionate. Jesus healed on the Sabbath; the father in the parable of the prodigal son had compassion on the son; and in the parable of the good Samaritan, the Samaritan, a member of a people much hated by the Jews, had compassion on the wounded robbery victim.

The discovery of ancient documents such as the Dead Sea Scrolls in the Qumran caves and other recent research have increasingly helped us understand the Palestine of Jesus' day—and how Jewish Jesus was. We now know Jerusalem to have been a much more cosmopolitan city than was previously thought, and Sepphoris, a town less than five miles from Nazareth, is now recognized to have been a thriving Hellenistic center. Such information helps us better locate Jesus in his time. The ruins of a leper's quarter in Bethany, a city a few miles to the southeast of Jerusalem, have been discovered. The Essenes and Pharisees were obsessed by the desire to avoid uncleanness; leprosy was the ultimate uncleanness. Imagine, then, the strength of—and the reaction of the religious leaders of Jesus' day to—Jesus' staying and eating at the house of Simon the leper in Bethany, mentioned in Mark 14:3.

Knowing the kind of thing Jesus did enables us to know him as a person. The core of such knowledge as we have described, a core common to the testimony of many witnesses, describes the singularity of a person and the communality of that person's life in time with our lives. Jesus is not a dead historic person confined to his times; he is a living person important in our time because he lives. Because Jesus lives and human times change, his Spirit will speak in different terms in different times, but the *kind* of life people are led to in the Spirit will always have the consistency of the *kind* of life Jesus lived on earth. That the Word of God is heard in Jesus of Nazareth does not mean that people can hear God's Word and live it only in the setting of first-century Palestine. Disciples of Jesus live the kind of lives in their time that Jesus lived in his. Words reported to be Jesus' do not specifically answer all the questions we can frame in the words of our day, but the life of Jesus is a life in which we can participate in our day in the Spirit. To acknowledge Jesus as the Christ does not make new problems go away, and faith in Jesus does not supply us with answers to problems before they arise.

Jesus did not come into the world to announce that things were about to be finished off in a manner removing us from total involvement in the creative work of the Spirit in time. Even if that is what Jesus consciously thought, it would but testify to the fact that he was truly located in his time as we are in ours; it would not destroy the efficacy of what God did in him. In Jesus and in the gift of the Spirit, God introduced something new into the dynamic order of his creation which must develop and grow in time. To be a disciple of Jesus is not to be given eternal laws from outside time—answers to our problems—that must be statically held in time no matter what happens, thus negating time; to be Jesus' disciple is to be an agent of love and humanization in all of one's relations with others in the Spirit in time. Jesus gives us his Spirit, in whom all things are to be made new, not a new Law by which to measure either ourselves or others.

The reign of God should not be expected to grow in a linear, straight-line fashion; that is not how God shows himself to work in the universe. The dynamics of God's continuing creation are more complex and interrelated than was simplistically thought in the past. Understanding the growth of the kingdom in the world in terms of the dynamic equilibrium of a sensitive system offers us encouragement where we would otherwise find discouragement. We see that everything we do everywhere is important. Such an understanding furnishes the reason for our continuing effort and witness on behalf of the kingdom at all times and in all places, no matter how discouraging things may look to us at the moment.

Whenever we follow the creative promptings of the Spirit, we inject a new initial condition in reality from which something else new may arise. We never know where our most influential witness to Christ will be made; due to the all-inclusive interrelations of reality, it can turn out to be made anywhere—so it must be made everywhere.

Weather forecasting offers an illustration of the attempt to make predictions in such a dynamic network of interrelations sensitive to initial conditions as we have been describing. New discernment of the complex network of atmospheric interrelations known as the weather system has led to the discovery of what is known as the "butterfly effect": a butterfly flapping its wings in China may introduce such a new initial condition in the atmospheric network that it will result in a thunderstorm in New York a month later.

In Christian tradition, the butterfly is a symbol of the resurrection. As we have just indicated, a Christian following the promptings of the Spirit of the risen Christ may inject such a new initial condition into the interconnected web of created reality as will have consequences for the growth of the kingdom of God in the world as great as the Chinese butterfly has for New York's weather. It is the Christian butterfly effect.

The circuity of the systems operating in historical reality make linear prediction difficult—often impossible—but the total interdependence of the sensitive networks whose dynamics constitute the universe maximizes the potential significance of the smallest unrepeatable action wherever it may occur. Everything and anything may be crucial. Nothing can be ruled out ahead of time as meaningless or useless; witness to Christ is important for the future of the world and for all creation.

What we have said up to this point may help us understand the growth of God's reign in the world in terms of our best understanding of the world today, and it may help us see the singular importance of the historical Jesus in the lives we live today. But if our efforts have been successful, the success has been achieved by overkill in the eyes of some, thus raising new problems. If Jesus plays the absolute role in our lives we have described, what about people who do not know or accept him as the Christ? What about the relation of Christianity to other religions? We live in a pluralistic world; if Jesus is the singular incarnation of the Word of God, where did other religions come from and what value do they have? Is it not arrogant and presumptuous to make absolute claims for one's particular point of view?

An increasingly recommended manner of responding to religious pluralism by Christians is the suggestion that Christians should realize that, when they call Jesus the Son of God or God incarnate, they are using a subjective language of love and commitment rather than making an objective statement everyone ought to acknowledge. John Hick has suggested that when a Christian says Jesus is his Savior, the statement has the same standing as a lover's statement that his beloved is the most beautiful woman in the world. Logically there may be one woman who is the most beautiful in the world, but who can judge among the claimants in their lovers' eyes?

To say that Jesus is the Son of God, the Messiah, is to say that Jesus plays an absolute role in the life of the person making the statement; it is an expression of personal love. The statement describes one person's experience, but it is said by Hick not to be a literal claim about a reality everyone should be expected to recognize.

Can one be a Christian in the sense we have described and then relate to the other religions of the world in the relativistic manner just commended? Can a Christian say that Jesus is the best source of his or her self-understanding, and in so saying mean that a different person's different religion is no doubt the best source of self-understanding for that person? A Christian cannot, if he or she is truly a witness to Christ. A witness can only witness to what he or she knows, and a witness must make his or her witness everywhere to everyone. A person who is nothing but a witness can be no more than a witness—and no less.

For a Christian meaningfully to say that Jesus is the best source of his or her self-understanding, the believer must have made an adequate sampling of other religions and judged Jesus to be best for him or her. In such a case, however, we must beware of Jesus being used as a means of achieving the believer's goal, rather than Jesus being the one who saves the believer from himself or herself. Jesus employed as the *means* of my self-understanding is not *the* Jesus! There is an element of election, of being chosen, in Christian love over which the believer has no control and which completely subordinates the believer to the love of the God who chooses him. To lose total dependence on God is to lose everything Christian. Such dependence is exactly what is lost if we think statements of our faith are only statements about how we function, rather than being descriptions of a reality upon which we—and everyone else—depend.

Jesus, the Word of God made flesh, is God calling our name. In Jesus, God speaks to us first; God speaks on his own initiative and there is nothing we can do about it. In a most important sense, the fact that we can do nothing about it is the most important thing about it. We can only hear; we can only listen.

God speaking to us first is God's choosing of us. It is by his mercy that we exist. "You did not choose me, but I chose you," Jesus says to his disciples. (Jn. 15:16) The point is made in different words in the First Letter of John: "We love, because he first loved us." (4:19) God is love, and in that love the Father speaks the Son as Word; through that same Word the heavens were made. When the Word speaks our name we are recreated; we are taken into the intimate life of God when we hear our name spoken by Jesus as Jesus. "As the Father has loved me, so have I loved you; abide in my love." (Jn. 15:9) God does not just tell what his life is like by his Word, he invites us into his life by his Word.

A witness can only be himself or herself when witnessing. The relativization of Christianity we have been examining has arisen because of the offensiveness to others of people who claim they are Christian witnesses. In the name of such witness, nonbelievers have been looked down upon and told they were condemned to hell. While such judgments may have been made by people who claim they are Christian witnesses, such judgements are not intrinsic to Christian witness. Christian mission to the world is necessary so that the joy of Christians may be fulfilled, as I John 1:4 indicates, not so that other people will escape everlasting punishment. Just punishment is proportionate to responsibility; where there is no responsibility there is no punishment. People who have not heard of Christ will not be punished for not accepting him. It is so obvious that it is a shame to have to mention it.

When Christian witness is made with one's life, instead of with words condemning others, the constancy of the witness is not offensive. The helplessness of a true witness to a mystery beyond him or her has an innocence which is its protection against offensiveness. Jesus is a mysterious witness to a mysterious God. In the Spirit we participate in the mystery; we do not solve it. Witnesses to God's mystery in Christ must not replace God; they must witness to God's judgement as they understand it, but they must not replace his judgement with theirs.

God's Spirit has been moving in the world since its beginning, and, in that Spirit, God's work is even now going on in the world beyond the boundaries of the visible church. We will have more to say about that in the next chapter. Karl Rahner introduced the concept of the "anonymous Christian" to describe a person who either had never heard of Christ or who consciously disbelieves that Jesus is the Christ, but who nevertheless is committed to the values Christians understand to constitute the kingdom of God. Rahner's term has come in for harsh criticism in recent years, for it is said to be insulting to call people anonymous Christians who explicitly deny they are Christians.

One person can never adequately speak for another, but speaking for myself I can say that, if a Hindu or a Muslim called me an anonymous Hindu or Muslim, as Rahner uses the term "anonymous," I would find nothing offensive in it. I would understand the remark to be a statement of witness on the speaker's part, rather than a denial of my identity. I do not know how else one could be a witnessing Hindu or Muslim. As Hindus, Muslims, and Christians live together making their mutual witness, all should be willing to leave final judgements in the hands of God. In who else's hands can they be in, if one believes in God? For the present, human beings should be all they can be in the Spirit wherever they are with whomever they are. To be offended by such presence and witness is to be offended by God, who allows such things to go on in his evolving creation.

12.

Back to the Beginning

Because we totally depend on Jesus in the beginning, we totally depend on him in the end. But our dependence should be better understood in the end than in the beginning. Trust is a basic attitude of human life, and there is no ultimate substitute for it. Because of the temporal nature of human life, the mind of Christ is a journey, not a possession.

We may now return to the beginning, to the simple acceptance of Jesus, but to such an acceptance cognizant of the world today and not naively offered.

Albert Einstein once said that everything should be made as simple as possible, but not simpler. Every Christian believer relates to Jesus simply. In the end, Jesus must be either accepted or rejected; there is no middle ground between the two in which *he* can be known. To be a disciple of Jesus in any age is to accept him as the Christ, but to be a disciple today is to accept Jesus in our world, not in a world of bygone days. The simplicity of accepting Jesus as the Way to the Father offers us a release from the complexity of our world, but it has necessary consequences in our world. Accepting Jesus as God's revelation of himself does not simplify our world by removing us from it; instead, it gives a constancy of God's presence to us, so that we can make a difference in the world in that presence.

It has been suggested that Jesus should be de-emphasized in Christianity and that Christians should be more concerned about God than Jesus. The "symbol of Jesus" at the heart of Christianity is said unnecessarily to limit people in their approach to God. Instead of revealing God, according to such a view, Jesus gets in the way of God, parochializing God and unnecessarily locating knowledge of God in a culture of the past.

It has been our contention that the more Jesus is located in his time the more he will help us in our time. We have been talking about the centrality of time in our lives, in Christianity, and in our lives as Christians. We have acknowledged that our lives as persons are temporal and that, in Jesus, God's truth entered time in the sense of itself becoming temporal. In the gift of the Spirit, we are able to live time as Jesus did. Life in the Spirit of the resurrected Christ is our participation in the resurrection, and it is the means of our being agents of the kingdom of God in the world.

That Christianity has not always been understood as we have been led to understand it cannot be denied. But that Christianity was misunderstood, when viewed differently, we have tried to show. Understood as we have tried to present it in these pages, we believe Christianity is viable and challenging in the world today. It is not a relic of a bygone age.

Because Jesus lives, he is relevant to every age—which means every age will understand him relative to the means available to it. Understanding Jesus in different ways is not the destruction of Christianity, such understanding is the foundation of Christianity, for different Christologies are found in the New Testament itself. But understanding Jesus as the Christ in a new way must not lead to a new Jesus. As we have seen, it is our sharing the very faith of Jesus that saves us, not our faith in Jesus. Growth in understanding Jesus' significance in changing times will not be tension-free, but that does not make such growth impossible. The ecumenically accepted creeds and conciliar definitions of Christian faith from the past, do not explain how God uniquely revealed himself in Jesus. The commonly accepted formularies of the past do not explain God for us; they rather state, in the terms available to them, that God did certain things that were witnessed in the world. The formulas serve as descriptive witnesses to an action that cannot be accepted as less than they describe, but the descriptions are not themselves the action they describe or the only description that may be possible of that action.

Jesus plays an essential and unsubstitutable role in Christianity, and Christianity continues as that same Jesus challenges us today. There is no substitute for, or better help to us than, Jesus, for it is only he who, as the Spirit-filled Christ, allows us to live victoriously in time as he does. Christianity, we said, started as the Jesus movement. The dependence of the movement on Jesus is also indicated by Josephus, a first-century Jewish historian, who, in his *Antiquities*, refers to Jesus' disciples as "the tribe of Christians." The identity of Jesus' followers was so completely one with the Messiah they confessed that they were known by his name even by those who did not believe as they did.

A great deal has been made in recent theology about the difference between a sign and a symbol. A sign refers to something totally beyond itself, while a symbol is said to refer to something beyond itself and also to participate in the thing it signifies. A sign that says "Refreshment Ahead" is not itself refreshing, but the flag of a country, for example, is a symbol of the country, because, in addition to referring beyond itself to the country, it is identified with the country in the reverence paid it. Even if the understanding of a symbol, as we have just described it, is granted, symbol is too weak a term to describe the presence of God in Christ. God's Word is one of a kind, and other words can adequately neither explain it nor illustrate it. The incarnate Word, because it is spoken by the creating God, brings a new type of personal presence with it.

Christianity has, on occasion, suffered from an overemphasis on Jesus which has led to Christomonism. Jesus has sometimes been so stressed devotionally or theologically that the deepest insight of Christian faith, the trinitarian life of God, has been eclipsed. In the understanding of Jesus we have presented, that cannot happen, for, as we have understood the role of Jesus, the life of the Trinity is revealed *in* him, not *by* him. We know Jesus in the Christian witness made to him only as the Son of the Father filled with the Spirit. The life of Jesus is the presence of the triune God; his life is not a sign pointing beyond itself to a God totally outside of it. To know Jesus is to know God and to be refreshed by God. Jesus is not a sign indicating God's refreshment to be somewhere else; Jesus is the presence of God's compassion—he is the presence of God's life—in the world. Jesus is God incarnate; he is God *here*.

To try to find God beyond the world is completely to miss the God of love who wants us to know him in the love he expresses for us, instead of in the way we seek him in order to satisfy the needs we feel. The difference is between knowing God as God reveals his inner life to us and knowing about God based on the needs we recognize in ourselves. In God's love our needs change; that is why life in the Spirit is our recreation.

We have frequently referred to Jesus, as he refers to himself in John's Gospel, as the Way, but to be with Jesus as the Way is not to think about Jesus—it is to be doing the will of the Father in the Spirit with Jesus. If we are with Jesus as his followers, we will pay attention to what he pays attention to, and we will do what he does. Under those circumstances, it is hard to see how a Christian could pay too much attention to Jesus' complete dependence on the Father.

Because Jesus is the Way, he does not get in the way. The Christian claim is that intimate knowledge of God is possible for us only through the life of Jesus, a life both lived and recognized in the gift of the Spirit. The Son and the Spirit are always with us, Christians believe, in our relations with God; they are the means the incomprehensible God of love uses to make himself knowable in our lives. *With* Jesus *in* the Spirit we are brought into the presence of the One who sent them.

The situation may be compared to our meeting someone we do not know, but whom we would like to know, who gives a party. We have heard about the person and we have always wanted to meet him, but, in addition to not knowing him, we do not even know where he lives. We do not know how to locate him. Happily, the person we want to meet is a friend of a friend of ours, and, because the unknown person wants us to meet him, he asks our mutual friend to bring us to his party.

We go to the party with someone we know to meet someone we do not know. In addition to showing us where the host lives and where the party is being held, going to the party with someone is different from going to the party alone. At the party, we meet the host, but we meet him in the presence of the person with whom we came and upon whom we depend for an introduction; the person's presence with whom we came makes a difference and is felt by us, but it is the person whose party we came to whom we see and upon whom we fix our attention. The presence of the person we came with is the context for meeting the person we came to see.

So it is with the Son and Holy Spirit; with them we concentrate on God the Father. They are with us, but it is the Father and his will upon whom we fix our attention. They "show" us how and where to be with the Father: the Spirit shows us *how,* and the Son shows us *where.*

It is impossible for a Christian to think he or she can get closer to God by getting around Jesus. If we can get to know God better within our own discretion than through Jesus, when we do turn to Jesus for the use he can be to us, he will be able to do no more than confirm what we said without him. That is very different from God coming to us and saying something new to us in Jesus. Jesus is the Word made flesh because, in his life, God says something he never said before; the alternative is that we speak the word of God and Jesus is our echo.

The life of Jesus is the perfect human life for a Christian. Does that statement mean Jesus is perfect because he is everything we are not, or does it mean he is everything we are—or are at least called to be? We have found him to be humanly perfect in his faith, not perfect in the sense that he needed no faith, thereby escaping the human condition. Jesus' perfection consists in his total dependence on the Father.

As we have understood it, Christianity is true because it happened; it did not happen because we could know it to be true. Since Christianity's truth depends on something that happened, we have to let it happen to us before we can know whether or not it is true. The reason for accepting Jesus as the Christ is the witness of others, not our personal needs. We should not think Christianity too good to be true because it fills our needs, but we must recognize its truth independently of the needs we feel at the moment. That is why it is so important to see the gospel, the good news that Jesus is the Christ, as personal communication rather than a book. Personal communication is immediately tied to the trust one has in a witness who is present; the source and motive of a book handed to us are unknown. The trustworthiness of a witness is one with the identity of the person confronting us.

Trust is a difficult relationship in our day. Many people's trust appears to have been buffeted and disappointed so many times in so many ways in our society that they, for their own protection, adopt a skeptical attitude for their approach to almost everything in life. A reserved, skeptical attitude is taken to be the mark of worldly wisdom; it is protection against credulity. It prevents one from being taken in, and it is touted as the hallmark of the scientific outlook.

Actually, trust is the first impulse of our lives, and if that impulse is frustrated, nothing else can substitute for it. Our first natural relationship with others is a trusting one, because, as we are born into this world, we are totally dependent on others. We know others before we know ourselves, and our first knowledge of ourselves comes from the way others treat us. If our initial trust is betrayed, we may need to subject our tendency to trust to scrutiny, but trust can never be produced by anything prior to it or more certain than it. Our first act—and our last act—is always acceptance; doubt is a secondary reaction. The very act of doubt supposes trust as its condition.

We have said the only way we can know whether or not Jesus is Christ and Savior is to trust him as *my* Savior. We can know nothing about him as Savior in general if he is not my Savior, for the salvation he brings is something that happens in our lives, not a theory about our lives.

Trust in Jesus is the first incisive´ personal relation we can have with him, just as trust is the first incisive relationship we can have with any person as a person. But more must be said about the way we relate to Jesus as Savior than that.

Paul made much of life "in Christ," and the misapplication of that phrase has sometimes led the church to misunderstand its role in the world. No biblical phrase or model can properly be removed from its context and absolutized as *the* key to our life with God. God's presence exceeds all of our words and thought forms, so we must take even biblical descriptions on balance when we accept the Bible, as we said we should, as the norm of the Christian experience of God.

We must not be misled when, in reading Paul, we think of ourselves "in Christ." We are never in Christ in the sense of being simply identified with him. To be "in Christ" means to be *with* Jesus *in* the Spirit. Jesus is the Christ because he is filled with the Spirit. We do not "enter" Jesus; Jesus comes to be with us and to lead us as the pioneer of our faith. He does not come to be invaded by us. When we live with Jesus, however, we are moved by his Spirit, and it is in that sense that we are "in Christ."

Paul speaks of the church as the body of Christ in the world, but the church is not simply Christ's body in the world. The church is Christ's body only so long as, filled with the Spirit, it follows Christ, not thinking it is he. Jesus' own words to Simon and Andrew, repeated to Levi the tax collector, were, "Follow me." (Mk. 1:17, 2:14) Another way of making the point in Paul's own terms is to say that the members of the body known as the church must not mistake themselves for the head of the body. It is important that the church understands itself to follow Jesus *in* the Spirit, rather than thinking it so has the mind of Christ in the world that it is simply able to do what Christ does *by* the Spirit. The church must constantly remind itself that only the historical Jesus is the Christ; the definitions of the church about Jesus as Christ do not replace Jesus or modify our dependence on his historical existence. Human definitions of the Christ—even when guided by grace—are not really definitions; they are descriptions. They describe what Christian faith believes God did in Jesus; they are not explanations of how God did it. The church does not make Christ, and it does not replace Christ.

For any member of the church to think he or she is in Christ with a simple identity destroys the essential temporality of being human; simply to identify ourselves with Christ makes us one with the source from which time flows instead of recognizing that our being is constituted by time. God's Word always comes to us from beyond us; thus it can be heard by us only as a call to move beyond where we are. If we act as if we are so in Christ that there is nowhere else to go, we make decisions that are not ours to make. We will have a false sense of security about where we are and surreptitiously divinize our status quo. A simplistic identity of the church with Christ has led to triumphalism in the church; it has led to the false identity of the church with the kingdom of God; and it has tried to make human decisions absolute in the name of Christ. The recognition that the church is a pilgrim church in the world by Vatican II was a partial recovery of the temporal dimension of our life in Christ to which we are referring. The recognition was a step in the right direction, but it is a direction in which many more steps need to be taken.

A Christian is a disciple of Jesus as the Christ, someone who follows Jesus as the Messiah. Followers of Jesus will have decisions to make, but they must not confuse theirs with his. Jesus is always beyond us calling us out of ourselves to him.

To see the meaning of Jesus as a meaning totally confined to the past because the initial witness to him is from the past is to misunderstand the meaning of a past event. The meaning of any historical event is determined by what follows from the event as well as by what led up to it and seemed to culminate in it. How many times has an historical "solution" to one problem later been discovered to be the source of a new problem? Old peace treaties, which were thought to end wars, sow seeds for new wars; an author is found to have said more than he or she knew; a period of rest later turns out to be a source of new creativity. The meaning of Jesus—and of no one in history—is suddenly stopped and fixed at a moment.

Jesus both is and is not exactly what he was in Galilee. He was the one sent to inaugurate the reign of God in the world in a new manner. In that sense he brought the future into our present, but he also went on to a fuller glory and so do those who live in his Spirit. Christian life is an everlasting growth from glory to glory; it is a life of constant change. Heavenly rest is unending growth.

We have seen that the reign of God proclaimed by Christ is concerned with one thing above all else—the relation of people in the world to each other in the presence of God. God so loved the world that he sent his Son into the world. The church is not a separate entity, called out of the world to be itself; the church is the people of God sent into the world to change the world by living in the world as Jesus did. The gift of God's Spirit, the Spirit given by the risen Jesus to his disciples as part of the Easter event, is a gift offered to all people. Jesus' life of compassion is made available throughout the world by the gift of the Spirit, not by means of never-failing propositions or by the letter of a law.

In the messianic age, it was believed God's Spirit would be poured out on all flesh, as Peter, quoting the prophet Joel, reminded those gathered at Pentecost. (Acts 2:17) In the messianic age recognized by Christians, the church is different from the world at large only because the church is that portion of the world that recognizes the reconciling work of the Spirit going on everywhere in the world—something the rest of the world misses. Augustine, in fact, described the church as the world reconciled to God.

The church is not different from the world because it *possesses* Christ or possesses grace the world lacks. The church is different from the world only in its knowledge of what God's purpose in the world is; that knowledge, achieved by God's covenant with his people through Jesus in the Spirit, should enable the church to cooperate with God's will for the world more completely. What a shame when it does not! The church is meant to lead the world into the future God has for it, but the church can so lead only if it follows Jesus.

The gift of the Spirit enables us to live Jesus' compassion and concern for others, but the Spirit does not enable the church to overtake Jesus and live with a certitude he did not have in his own life. Jesus is recognized as Lord and Savior because of his resurrection from the dead; he was not proclaimed Lord because he was infallible and never made a mistake. The best knowledge we have of Jesus indicates he was mistaken about who wrote the psalms, and he seems to have been wrong, John's Gospel apart, about the imminence of the second coming. Jesus is proclaimed Lord and Savior only because he rose from the dead. He is Lord because of his indefectibility, not his infallibility. In the Spirit his life did not fail, and, following him in the Spirit, our lives will be upheld in God's love too. With the assurance of the resurrected Jesus as their Way, followers of Jesus do not need more ability than Jesus himself had to achieve God's will and actualize the reign of God in the world.

There will be tension and struggle, problems and difficulties, as God's creation continues in the actualization of the kingdom. Progress will not always be visible, and a clear path will not always be seen; that is the way we have discovered creation to proceed in the evolution of the dynamic system called the universe. The important thing is that the universe is not a closed system and neither are our lives. To say that God created the universe is to say that the universe is itself only beyond itself: the world and we are not fulfilled within ourselves just by being ourselves. Both we and the universe are open to God's presence, and in that presence alone is our fulfillment.